Canon EOS 750/850

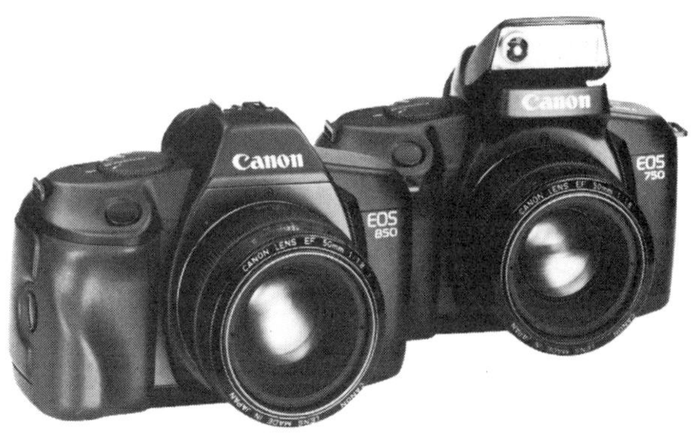

Thomas Maschke

HOVE ~ FOUNTAIN BOOKS

CANON EOS 750/850

First English Edition June 1989
English Translation: Liselotte Sperl
Series Editor: Dennis Laney
Technical Editor: George Wakefield
Editor: Georgina Fuller
Typeset by Brighton Typesetting, Sussex
Printed in West Germany by Kösel-Druck, Kempten

ISBN 0-86343-205-0
U.S.A.: ISBN 0-906447-53-4

Published by
HOVE FOUNTAIN BOOKS
the joint imprint of

Fountain Press Ltd   &   Hove Foto Books
45 The Broadway, Tolworth   34 Church Road, Hove
Surrey KT6 7DW   Sussex BN3 2GJ

U.K. Trade Distribution by
Fountain Press Ltd

Contents

Black Beauty

This is a camera that is not only pleasing to the eye but also to hold. The designers at Canon have taken great care to create a beautiful exterior while at the same time considering its functions. Like few other manufacturers they have been successful in combining a pleasing appearance with great ease of handling for the entire EOS series of cameras. Holding an EOS camera in your hand puts you at ease with your equipment. This is as it ought to be. After all, if you don't enjoy handling your camera you won't be able to take good pictures, but the EOS cameras are designed with the ultimate enjoyment of photography in mind.

EOS is a very poetic name for a technical instrument. Pleasantly so, compared with the general trend of coded abbreviations. No other well-equipped camera is as uncluttered with operating elements as the EOS. In this respect too, Canon are leading the way in the development of photographic equipment towards less complicated but still highly advanced technology to aid the photographer in his task. To be able to concentrate fully on the subject without being side-tracked by unnecessary manipulation of technical gadgetry, this is the ideal situation that has been realized with the EOS 750 and 850 cameras. The 620 and 650 models have already impressed the photographic world by the way they combine a minimum of operating elements with a wealth of facilities. This idea has been further developed with the 750 and 850 models where even more buttons and controls have been taken away. Switching on and off, this is more or less the only thing that the photographer has to do himself as far as camera manipulation is concerned. If you are using the 750, then even photography by integrated flash is automatic. If the lighting conditions require it the flash comes automatically into action and then folds away after use.

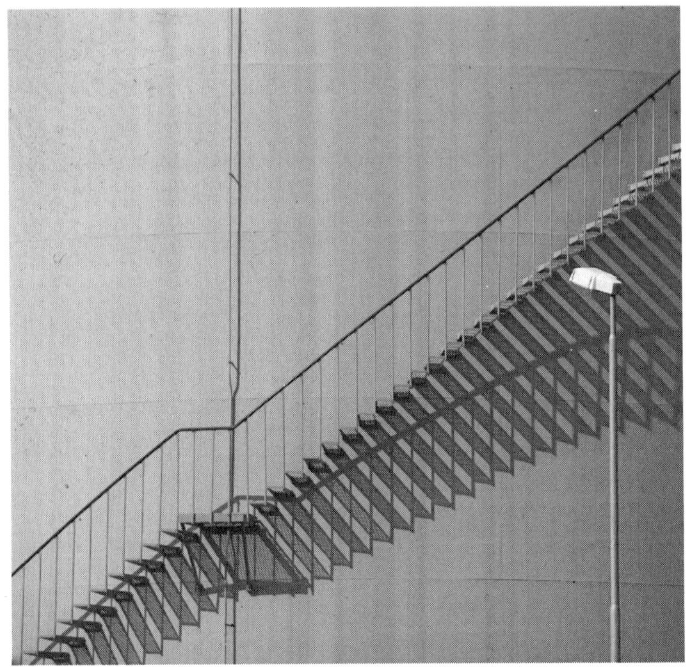

The interaction of light and shade is particularly impressive in black-and-white photography.

However, this apparent simplicity is deceiving. Behind the smooth exterior hides highly-developed electronic and optical systems. Sensors, microprocessors and motors control the camera's functions accurately but the photographer need not worry; the reduction in operating elements does not mean a loss in photographic facilities but more of a gain in faster and simpler handling.

The EOS models, which are the subject of this book, are obviously cameras for uncomplicated photography. Uncomplicated means that the photographer hardly needs to make any adjustments on the camera and that there is little room for error. This does not imply that one cannot take good pictures, quite the contrary; it leaves the photographer free to concentrate fully on the image without fear of accidentally pressing the wrong button.

Even the most sophisticated automatic mode has blind spots — areas where the thinking photographer can produce better results. I have made it my duty to supply you with a glimpse behind the scenes, to provide you with an insight into your EOS so that it doesn't remain a mysterious black box. Also being better informed usually means being able to achieve better results. You will be able to appreciate why some of your pictures turn out so well and others do not. The background knowledge is not only useful in appreciating why the automatic facilities perform less than perfectly in certain circumstances, but knowing this also makes it possible for you to achieve satisfactory pictures even in borderline situations. I do not intend to subject you to a lot of dull facts but hope that this book will constitute a lively and interesting course on the use of EOS cameras in particular, and photography in general, which will help you to take better pictures now and in the future.

Get to know how the camera works by holding it and trying out all the functions and you will realise that these are very sophisticated, with the "hit rate" being exceedingly high. Multi-field metering (Evaluative Metering as it is called by Canon) and automatic focusing reduce the likelihood of faulty shots to a minimum. Once you have mastered the few manipulations you can concentrate on the activity you bought the camera for — photography.

EOS - The Camera

Canon decided on a rather unusual policy with the development of their EOS series. Generally, camera manufacturers endeavour to distinguish their models clearly by the different facilities offered by each one. However, the differences between the 750 and 850 models are minimal. On the other hand Canon were able to offer several different camera bodies all based on the same basic camera design. The advantage of this solution is that the customer need not pay for any facilities that he does not really need or want. The disadvantage is, that it is not possible to convert an EOS 750 or EOS 850 into an EOS 750 QD (Quartz Data), as the camera back cannot be changed.

The coding for the autofocus generation of cameras is also different. The more facilities that are packed into a model, the lower the model number. Consequently, the EOS 850 with the highest number is the most spartan (if we can use this word in connection with an EOS camera) of the series. All three cameras; the 850, 750 and the 750 QD, are the same internally – differing only in additional facilities such as integrated fill-in flash and a data back.

EOS 850

The EOS 850 does not offer a flash, nor has it a data back and it is therefore the cheapest in the range. Otherwise, and I wish to emphasise this, the 850 is exactly the same as the EOS 750. It is identical in autofocus, multi-field metering and all other technical details and uses the same lenses, flashguns and accessories.

Canon even developed a small flashgun, the Speedlite 160E, which would be ideal for this model as a fill-in flash. Together with the small Speedlite, the EOS 850 offers the same facilities as the 750; however, the separate flashgun costs considerably more than the price difference between the two models. It is also not as compact as the integrated flash. Having a guide number of 12, it performs the same functions as the integrated flash of the two other models. From a creative point of view the EOS 850 with a flashgun offers the same automatic flash modes as the two EOS 750 models.

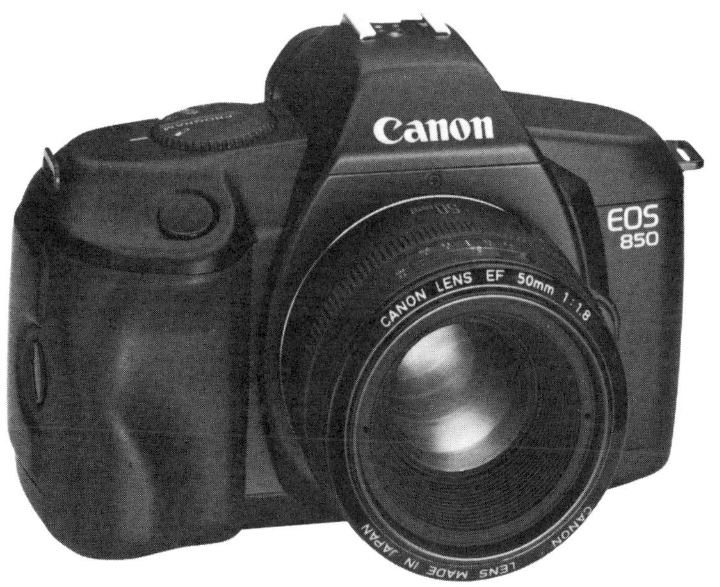

Photography could be defined as drawing with light and the EOS as a pencil. But the thoughts that are to be expressed, i.e. what is to be committed to film, are still the photographer's choice.

EOS 750

The EOS 750 is available in two versions. These differ from the 850 model by offering an elegantly-integrated flash unit. The output of this miniflash, with a guide number of 12, is not very high but is sufficient for fill-in flash in declining light. It is often the case that we need just this little bit extra to save the situation. A particularly attractive feature is the fully retractable flash. The program mode decides, completely unaided, whether the flash is necessary as fill-in for backlit shots or to boost the general lighting level. Whenever the camera recognizes this situation, the miniflash is swung up and comes into

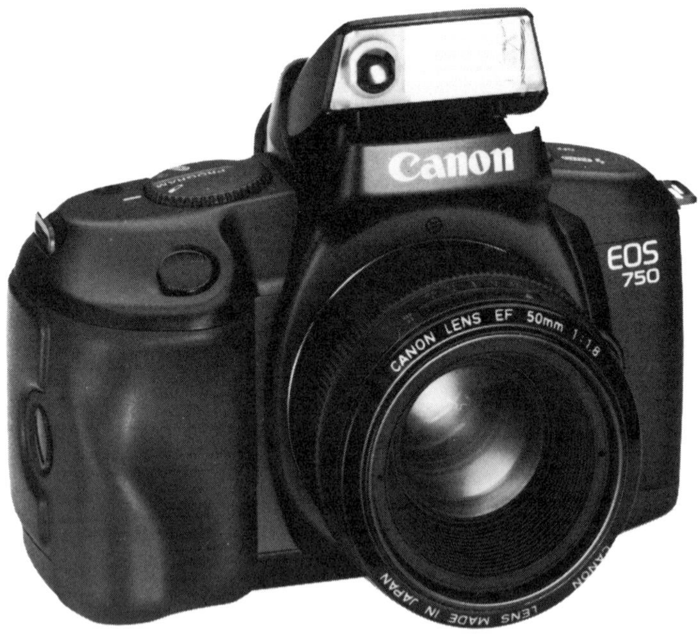

The integrated flash of the EOS 750 is particularly elegant. It automatically switches on when conditions demand. Otherwise it is folded away and completely invisible.

action when the shutter is released. After the exposure is made it automatically retracts into the camera housing. It is also possible to switch the flash unit off, in case you wish to make a long exposure without flash. The EOS 750 is the most compact alternative to a small additional flashgun as it neither spoils the appearance of the camera nor its handling.

EOS 750 QD

The EOS 750 QD is the twin to the EOS 750 in all aspects apart from the fact that it also possesses a special Data Back which enables the date and time of day to be exposed onto the negative. QD stands for Quartz Date, which indicates the integrated digital calendar and clock mechanism based on quartz control for absolute exactness. Quartz crystals vibrate at a very precise frequency which is measured in hertz. Technical quartz crystals have typical frequencies of 10,000 to 20,000 oscillations per second. These oscillations are counted by an electronic circuit in the data back. If the quartz used oscillates at a frequency of 20 kilohertz, then a full second is counted down after 20,000 oscillations. This results in the accuracy of quartz clocks. Any deviations amount to at most 90 seconds per month — a tolerance that a normal mechanical clock mechanism would have in one day.

Using the Data Back you can expose the day/month/ year in any preferred notation onto the negative, alternatively the day and time of day can be exposed. To be able to choose the notation is quite important. After all, we are not used to interpreting 12:10:88 as 10th December 1988. It is true, the photographer could get used to it, but anyone else will generally need explanations. The above notation is the one generally used in the U.S.A.. To avoid any incorrect interpretations the notation can be chosen to conform to the generally understood way; here in the United Kingdom we would select 10:12:88 which is

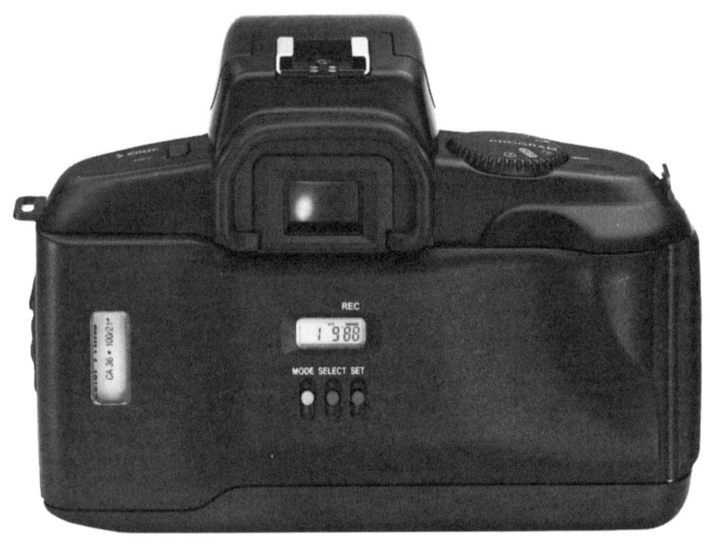

The EOS 750 QD has an integrated data back as a special facility. It allows the exposure of date, or day and time onto the negative.

generally accepted to mean 10th December 1988.

The display and exposure of data is via an LCD panel. It goes without saying that you can choose whether or not the date is exposed onto the film. Operation of the Data Back functions is really quite simple. The values to be changed are selected by **SELECT** button and the required value by the **SET** button. These two buttons will select the time and also the date. The **MODE** button is used to select the date notation or alternatively the day and time. The calendar of the EOS 750 QD Data Back is programmed from 1978 to 2019 and takes into account the lengths of the months and leap years.

How useful you think a data back will be depends entirely on your own preferences. In the case of slide films that are returned from the lab in mounts, the processing date will be stamped on the frame (this depends on the make of film used) allowing the slides to be identified, but

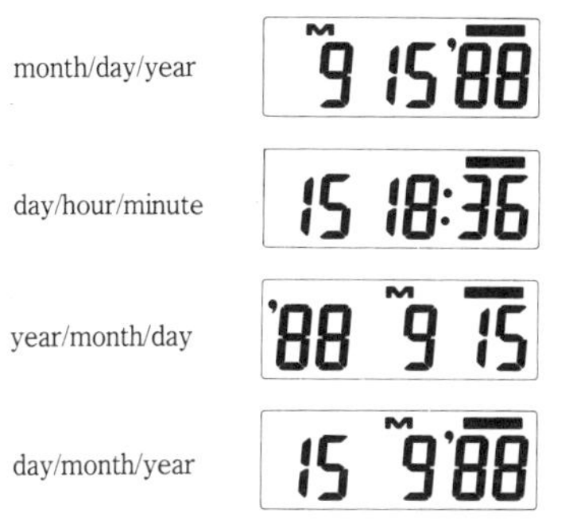

The selected data are shown on the LCD panel of the data back.

if you keep a film in the camera for a long time this will not be of much use! Even so, if you are interested only in the approximate date and usually use slide film, then you can save yourself the expense of a Data Back. However, if your medium is print film, then the facility could be quite useful. Whenever essential, or useful, you can show the date or time when the picture was taken on every print. To expose the time may be useful for events where the date is remembered (wedding, birthday), and the exposure of the time would place the shots in their chronological sequence.

Useful Facts About The EOS System

The three models are nearly identical as far as their interior and the operating elements are concerned. The only difference is that the two 750 models have an additional switch on the left of the penta prism housing and this is used to switch the integrated flash unit off and on.

The most important − and indeed the only − operating element of the EOS 750/850 cameras is the Selector Dial. This is used as a selector and indicator of the various functions. As mentioned previously, this is the first technically sophisticated camera with so few operating elements. This is in no way a disadvantage, but facilitates

The operating elements of the EOS 850/750:

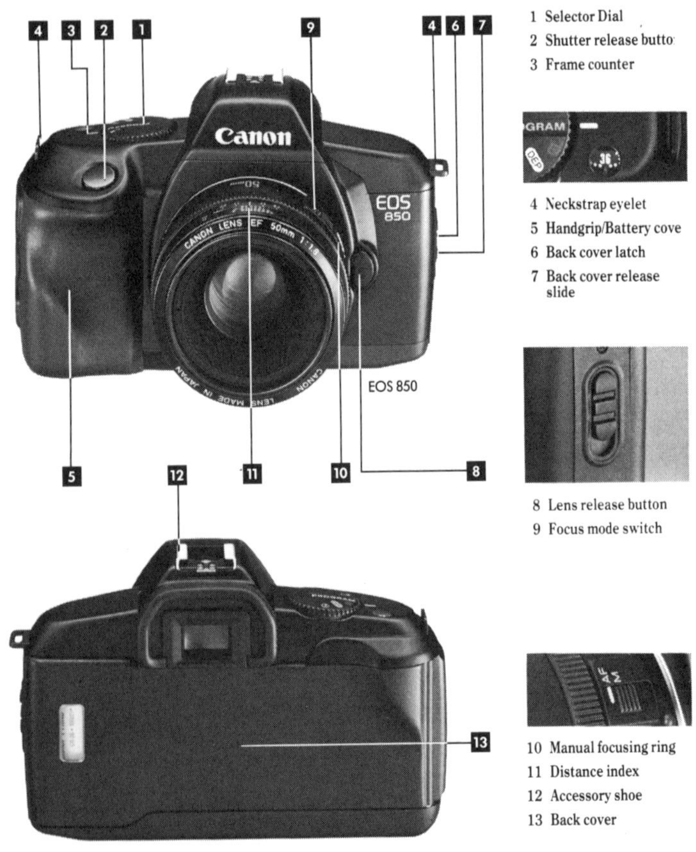

ease of handling. Simple handling does not mean simple technology and because this technology has been so fully developed and perfectly designed Canon were able to reduce the operating tasks to a few manipulations.

Which position corresponds to what function can be

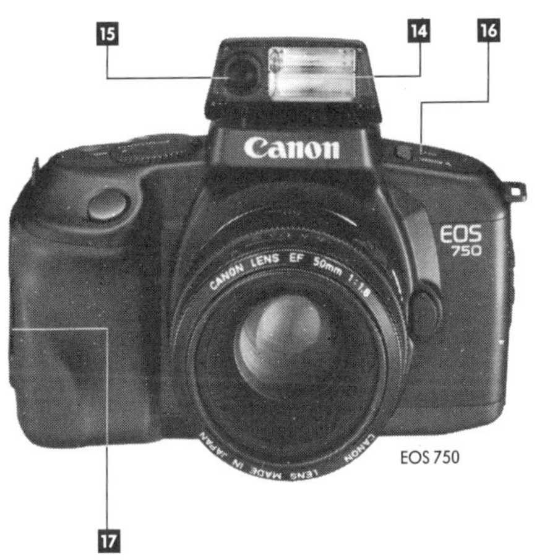

EOS 750

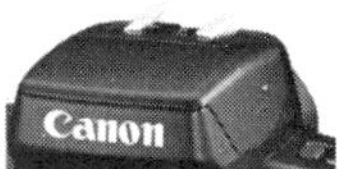

14 Flash head
15 Infrared light emitter

16 Flash switch

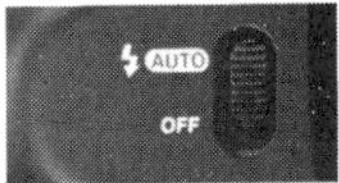

17 Grip screw
18 Tripod socket
19 Film-load check
   window
20 Date imprint function

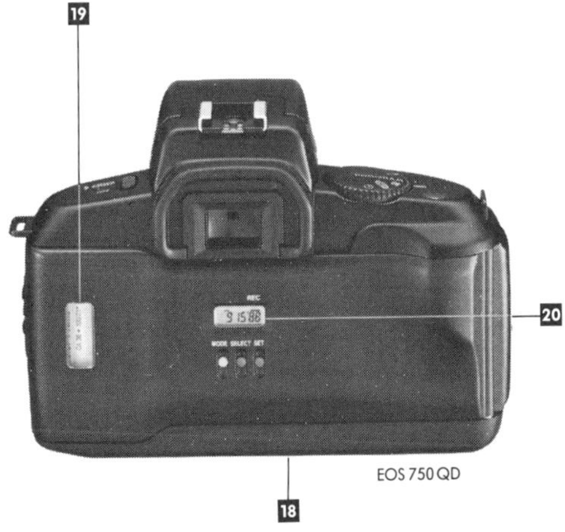

EOS 750 QD

seen from the camera's operating instructions. Battery check, camera on/off and self-timer are activated by the Selector Dial. An audible signal will warn you of insufficient battery power and if the film has been incorrectly loaded. Then you can select either of the two functions; program

17

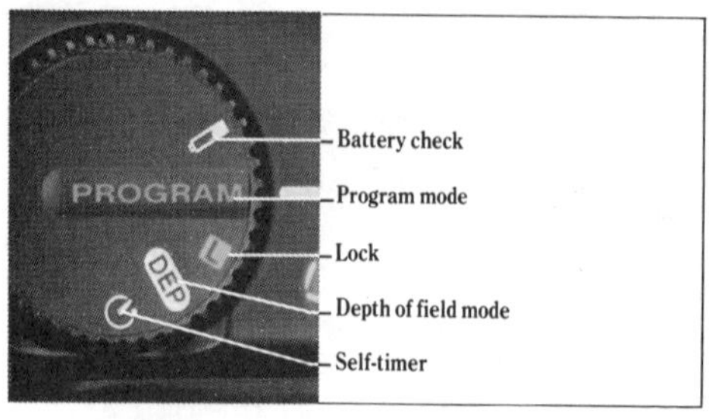

mode or depth of field mode. And that is the most important thing you will have to do to produce great pictures, ensuring perfect exposure and sufficient depth of field.

Here too Canon have come up with a special facility to more or less guarantee success for the widest range of situations. Understanding the exposure modes and their functions is so important that I have dedicated a whole chapter: *Practical EOS Photography I* to it where you can find more detailed information.

The release works on the "one shot" principle (as Canon calls it). This means a slight pressure on the release will cause the camera to meter and set the exposure and focus setting; pressing the release fully will make the exposure. If the autofocus is unable to find a point for sharp focus, then the release will be blocked. Exception: if the switch on the lens is set to **M** for manual focusing you can release any time. In this case it is possible to take completely unsharp pictures.

To perform these functions, the camera body houses not only a number of microchips and an "intelligent brain" in the form of programs, but also several motors that carry out the programmed instructions. Each lens has two motors; and then there are further motors for the autofocus. Another motor pulls the film out of the cassette after it has been inserted and yet another motor, situated on the other side, returns the exposed film, a frame at a time, back into the cassette.

No doubt you will have noticed that the time of awkward film loading is over. All you need do now is insert the cassette, pull the film leader out as far as the orange marker and close the camera back. The EOS then loads the film quite automatically. You will notice that the motor seems to be active for quite a while. This is because it pulls the film right out of the cassette and advances it to the last frame. This is a good idea which is quite easy to accomplish with motorized film transport, only nobody thought of it before. Other cameras, even the EOS 620, do this the other way round as is usual; the film is exposed in ascending order and returned into the cassette after the last frame is exposed. The new descending order brings about a few important advantages. Firstly it is safer; if the camera back should be accidentally opened then only unexposed film and perhaps the last exposed frame will be spoilt. The other exposed frames, that have been returned to the cassette, should be quite safe. Another effect is that now the frames are counted down and one can read off how many are left, which is generally more useful than knowing how many frames have been exposed.

Should the film not have loaded properly, then you will be warned by an audible signal. This will sound immediately when an unsuccessful attempt at film loading is made and you try to activate the release. You can also visually check this by reading the frame counter.

The EOS performs another function during film loading; it reads-in the film speed. This information is important for correct exposure metering. Most film cassettes now have a chessboard-like black and silver pattern, which is the code for the film speed, the DX-code. The contacts in the film compartment read this pattern and recognize the code for the speed of the loaded film. The EOS cameras are capable of reading film speeds from ISO 25/15° to ISO 3200/36°. Automatic reading-in of film speed is possible only in full stops, i.e. 25/15°; 50/18°; 100/21°; 200/24°; etc. If the film speed is an intermediate value, then the film

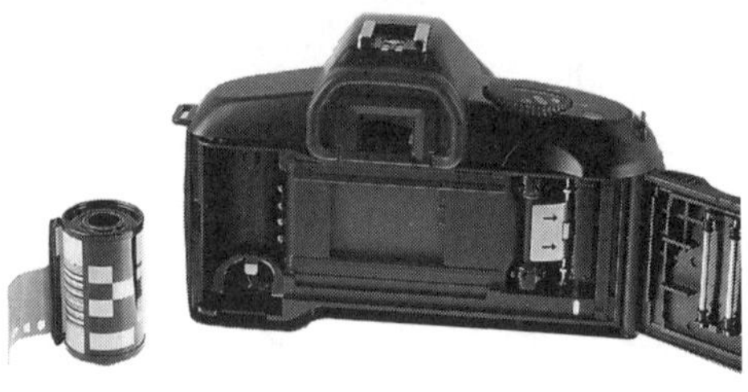

Contacts in the camera body recognize the speed of the loaded film by the pattern on the cassette which is automatically read into the camera computer.

may be incorrectly exposed with the error being as much as ⅔ of a stop. For example, the Ektachrome tungsten film ISO 160/23° which would be read as ISO 100/21°. This slide film would therefore be clearly overexposed so it is best to buy films that are rated in full stops which can be correctly recognized by the EOS 750/850 cameras. Colour print films can tolerate greater errors in exposure and a slightly incorrect film speed setting should produce quite acceptable results.

On the camera back you can see through the film-load check window to see if one is loaded. Most manufacturers print the make and speed at this point on the cassette in order that this information may also be checked. This ensures that you always know whether a film is loaded and what it is.

Once you have assured yourself that no film is loaded, you can open the camera back to inspect the details that make automatic film transport possible. The user of a modern camera soon comes to appreciate the semi-automatic film loading facility. It is most helpful not to have to perform all sorts of finger acrobatics, holding down the cassette, trying to thread the film leader into the slot ... Now film loading is easy — simply pull the film out of the

---

A camera with intelligent automatic mode, such as the EOS, frees the photographer from any bothersome technical burden. He can concentrate fully on the subject. However, he has to be able to recognize correct lighting and how to convert this into a good picture.

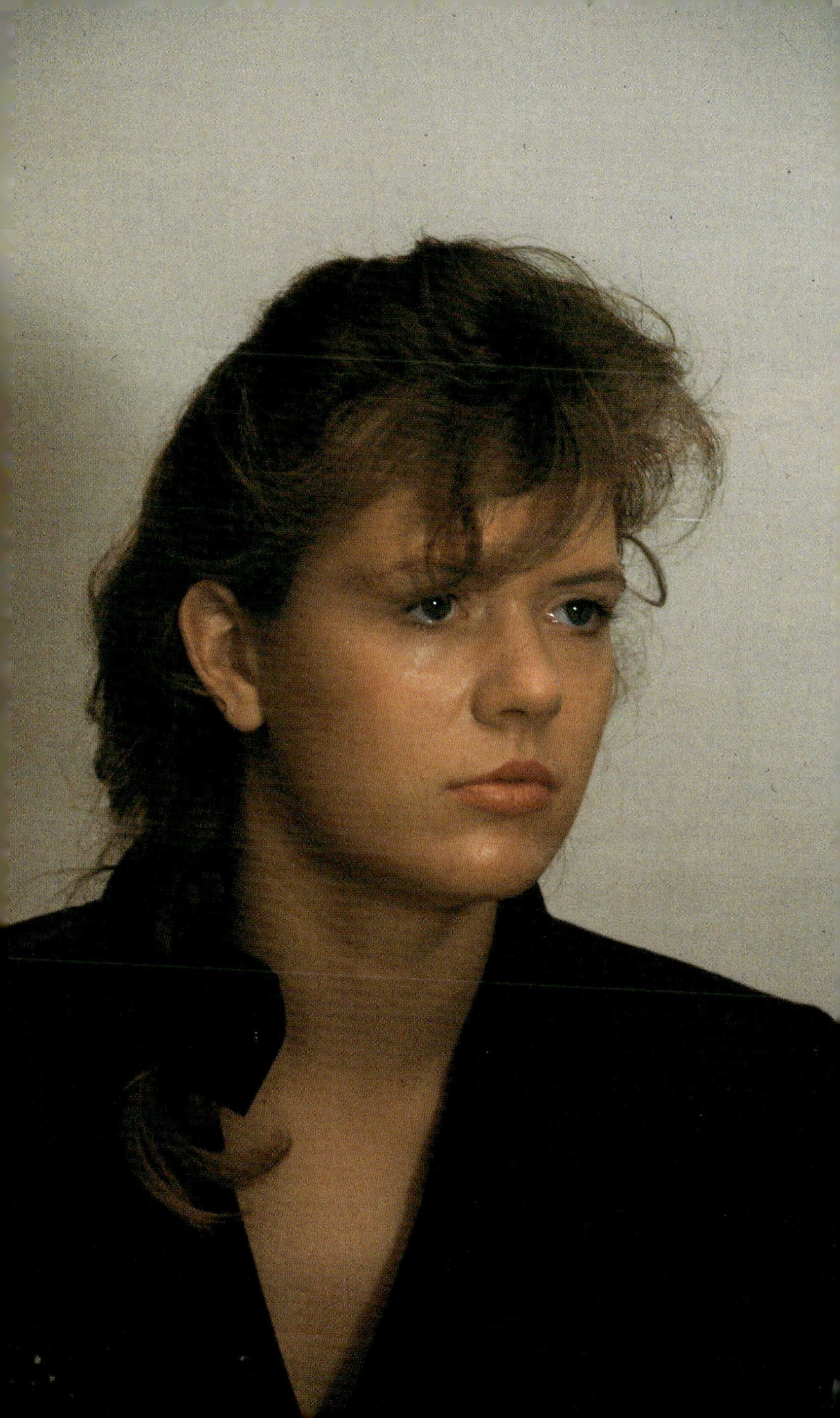

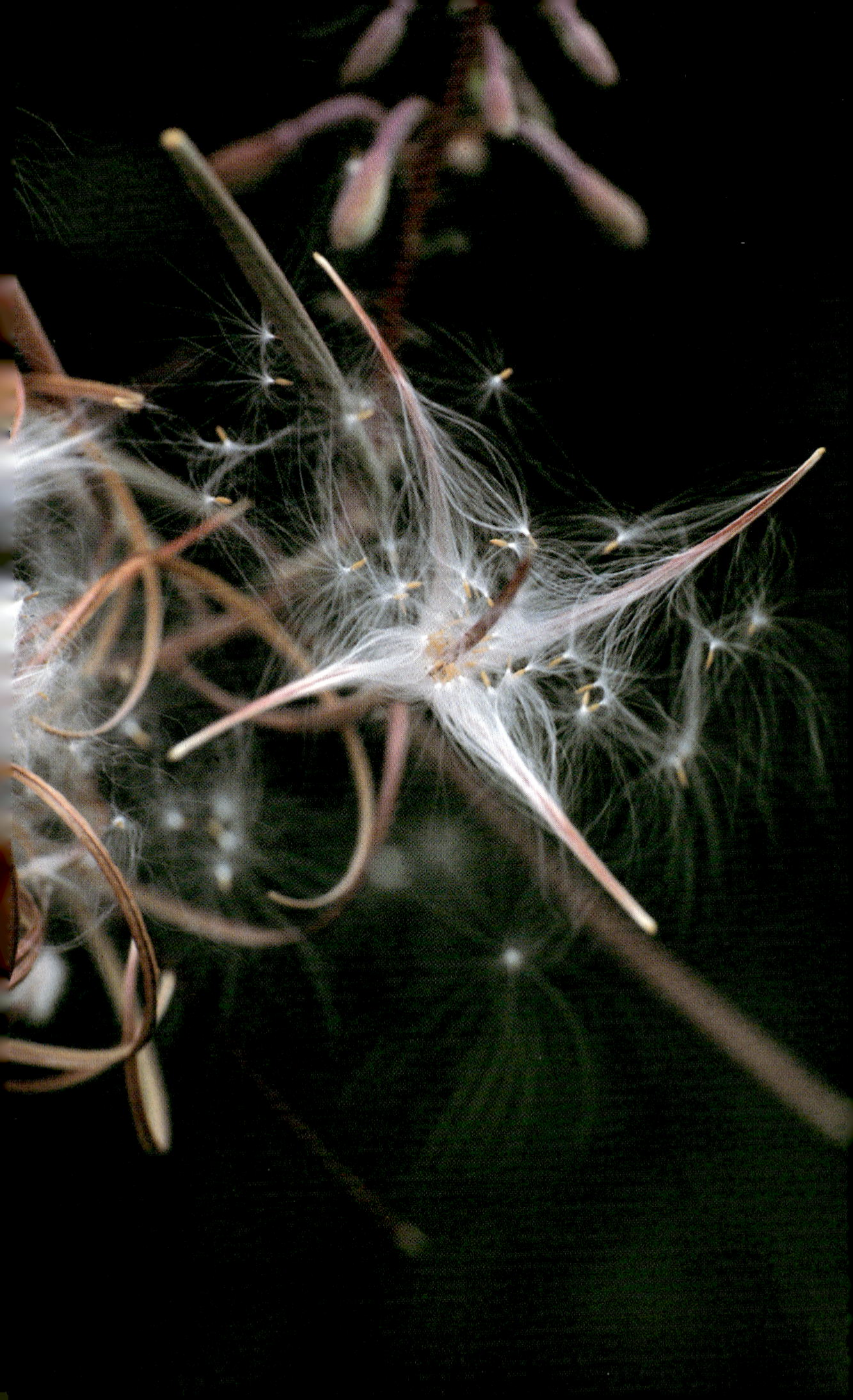

cassette as far as the orange marker, close the back panel and the EOS will do the rest quite automatically. But before you do this, have a look into the camera's interior. On the inside of the back panel is a sprung plate – the film pressure plate. This, together with the two film guide rails, ensures proper alignment of the film for each exposure. It is very important that the film is correctly positioned during exposure; even one hundredth of a millimetre distortion of the film could cause the image to be blurred in certain areas.

Between the two guide rails you can see the two shutter blinds which open for an accurately measured time during the exposure. To be precise, the blades travel vertically across the film plane. The EOS, like most other SLR cameras, has two shutter blinds, one of which moves across the film plane exposing the film to the light; the second follows after a period corresponding to the shutter speed that has been set. In the case of fast shutter speeds, e.g. $\frac{1}{1000}$ sec., the two blinds follow each other very quickly and the film is exposed by a slit moving across the film plane.

Precise control of the speed of the shutter blades is of the utmost importance, otherwise the film would not be uniformly exposed. To appreciate the demands on the mechanical engineering of a camera you should consider the function of the shutter more closely. The blinds are first accelerated at an extremely fast rate, then they move at as uniform a speed as possible across the film, to be abruptly braked at the other end. Because of the slight, but inevitable, inertia the speed cannot be kept absolutely

---

*Macro photography opens up an entirely new field. Everyday things that we normally pass without a glance become objects of beauty and interest. Sufficient depth of field was ensured by the depth mode and any danger of camera-shake would have been indicated by the flashing **P** in the viewfinder. In critical situations it is better to choose a larger aperture, as the shutter speed may become too slow with a small aperture and the picture would be blurred because of camera shake.*

constant across this very short distance and to compensate the width of the slit has to be varied to ensure uniform exposure across the whole frame. As the shutter increases its speed the width of the slit is constantly increased by the minutest amount so that the sum total of exposure at every point is constant.

After the shutter has completed its task it has to be brought back into its starting position. This is done immediately after the exposure has been made, simultaneously with the film being transported to the next frame. By the way, do be careful when loading a new film not to touch the shutter blinds as these are very delicate and thin to keep their inertia to a minimum for the extremely fast speeds that are made possible by modern camera technology.

Looking at the camera body you may notice that there is no connector for a remote release. This should present no problem as this function is just as easily performed by the electronic self-timer. For long exposures a tripod and remote release are usually used to avoid camera shake. In critical situations the pressure on the release can cause slight vibrations and thus camera shake. This has very noticeable effects even for relatively fast shutter speeds even if the camera is supported on a tripod.

Tip: If you are making a long exposure with the camera mounted on a tripod use the self-timer. This ensures that any movement after pressing the release will have ceased in the count-down period.

As you can see, the integrated self-timer is perfectly suitable for replacing the wire release. I would strongly recommend using it for all exposures whenever you use slow shutter speeds and a tripod.

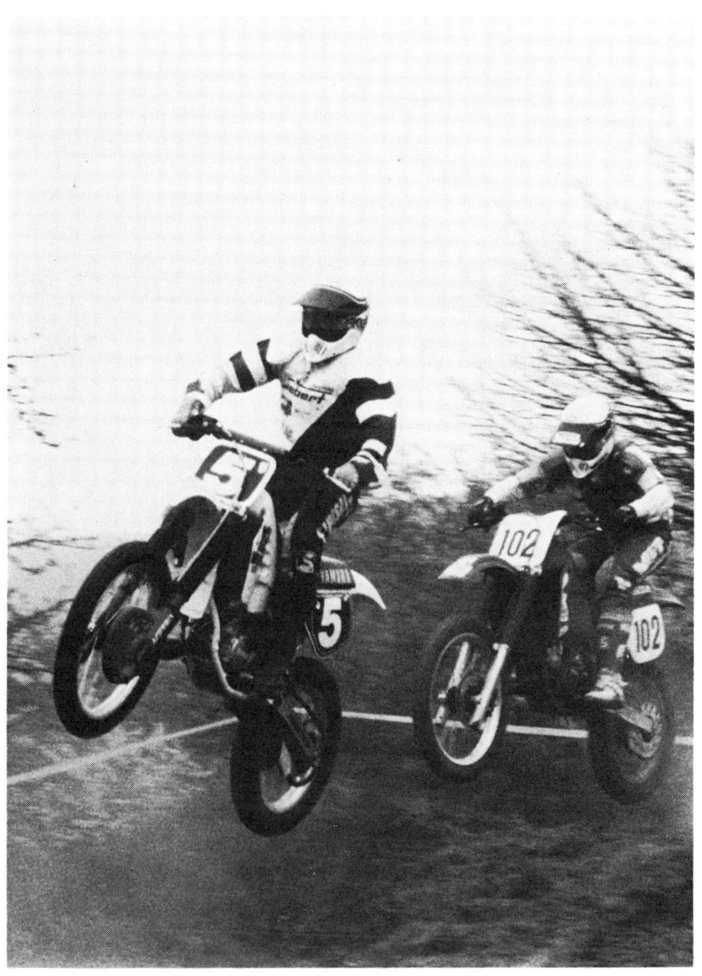

Safeguarding against camera-shake was very important in this shot. A flashing green **P** any time during the sequence will indicate that the lighting conditions are critical. A fast film (ISO 400/27°) was used to ensure a suitably fast shutter speed. The camera was panned in the direction of the movement to reproduce the cyclists sharply in the picture. The lens was set to manual focusing as the autofocus facility might not have been able to cope with the fast action.

Viewfinder Information

The first thing the experienced photographer notices when looking through the viewfinder is the very bright image. This is due to the excellent focusing screen. Removing the lens and looking straight into the camera you can see the reflection of the focusing screen in the mirror. Tilting the camera back you can also see the focusing screen at the top of the camera interior. It is the duty of the focusing screen to make visible the image that is projected through the lens. For some time now Canon have used special screens which are a great improvement on conventional matte screens. This new type of focusing screen is manufactured by a laser beam which results in a much finer, more uniform structure and, as a result, have higher transmission values and are therefore much brighter than conventional focusing screens and also has good definition to the very edges of the frame.

Please note that the viewfinder image only shows 92% of the actual picture area. This is intentional to permit some cropping in the final photograph.

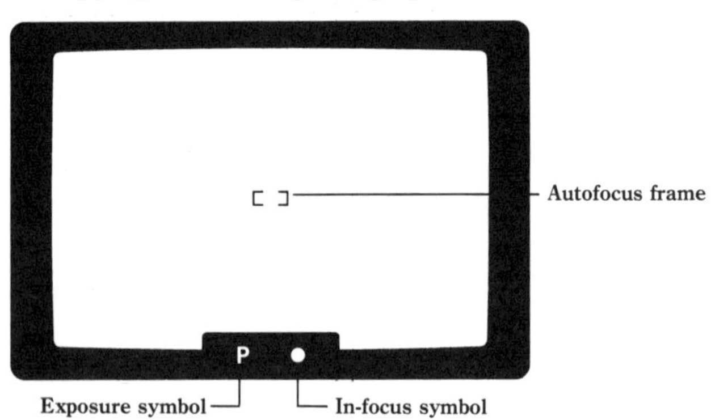

[ ] – point at the main subject
P   – illuminates if correct exposure is possible
P   – blinks for incorrect exposure or danger of camera-shake
●   – illuminates when autofocus for the subject is correct
●   – blinks if focus for the subject is impossible

The display in the viewfinder is as clearly laid out as the operating elements. One green dot; the In-focus Symbol, and a green **P**; the Exposure Symbol, which will, depending on the situation, light up constantly or blink. If the green dot flashes it means that the autofocus cannot produce a sharp focus and the release will be blocked. In this case you will either have to select a more suitable focusing point or change to manual mode and focus by hand.

The green **P** in the viewfinder deserves some mention. If this symbol flashes it means that there is danger of camera shake. This warning symbol is a very intelligent device; the electronic control recognizes what focal length lens is used at any given time and the green **P** will blink if the measured exposure time is up to half a stop slower than the reciprocal of the focal length of the lens in mm.

For example: let's assume that you are using a 100mm lens with the camera. The well-tried rule says that the shutter speed for hand-held shots should be no slower than $\frac{1}{100}$ sec. (1/focal length). If you find it difficult to appreciate why the critical shutter speed varies with the focal length of the lens, then think of binoculars. Looking at a distant object with the naked eye it appears quite sharp. Using powerful binoculars, the world begins to shake. To explain this − the binoculars not only enlarge the subject but also the viewer's own movements. The same happens when looking through a lens. The longer the focal length, the greater the magnification of camera movement. This gave rise to the above rule, which has proved very useful over the years.

The warning function of the EOS works exactly according to this principle. You should take note of this facility and change the lens if great sharpness is important. This is a good example of how modern technology can assist the photographer in producing better pictures. Formerly the display of the shutter speed was necessary to interpret the camera-shake warning in the viewfinder and you had to remember what focal length lens was attached to calculate the safe shutter speed for the shot. The display of the shutter speed is therefore quite superfluous in the case of the EOS 750/850, one glance at the **P** is sufficient to ensure that you are within safe limits.

Even if the attached lens is a zoom, the EOS keeps itself constantly informed as to the selected focal length and it is not necessary for you to take the camera from your eye to check the actual setting. If one considers that zoom lenses for focal lengths between 70-210mm are quite normal these days and that the resulting safe shutter speed varies between $\frac{1}{100}$ to $\frac{1}{250}$ sec. for this range of focal lengths, then we can appreciate how useful this intelligent warning system really is. This example serves to demonstrate quite clearly that it is often sufficient to simply adjust the focal length somewhat to change a blinking **P** into a constantly lit one; better a larger subject field than an unsharp picture.

One should remember that the electronic functions of the EOS are based on a general rule that has proved useful but not infallible. The basic provision is still only an approximate rule which has been taken as the basis for the warning function. Depending on the actual circumstances it may require much faster shutter speeds to obtain really sharp pictures. Just think of a child skipping. On the other hand, there are also situations where a much slower shutter speed will still produce a sharp image. Unfortunately, tales of absolutely sharp pictures, taken hand-held at 1 sec, should be taken with the proverbial pinch of salt.

It is better to use the above formula or to increase it by taking twice the focal length to be on the safe side. This does not mean that you cannot expose under any circumstances when the blinking **P** warns you of camera shake. On the contrary, consider the situation and shoot away but be aware that you will most probably not be able to keep the sharpness in big enlargements. The warning should make you look for some sort of support for making the exposure. It may be sufficient to use your own body, pressing your arm against your chest or better still against a bent knee. Then there are always such objects as a wall, a bannister, or the roof of a car that could serve the same purpose.

If a flashgun is attached and switched on, then the **P** flashes in a similar manner to indicate that the flashgun is not yet charged. As soon as the flash is ready the **P** will be constantly lit.

Tips/Conclusion: The green **P** in the viewfinder is a very important display and the following should be remembered:

○ When shooting, if the **P** flashes occasionally and then only if the subject is situated in a shady area, the available light can be assumed to be bright enough to photograph freely without worrying too much about camera shake.

○ If you are using a zoom lens (e.g. the 70-210mm) and the warning is given repeatedly when the zoom is set to 210mm, but not at the shorter focal length of 70mm, then the lighting conditions are close to the critical level. The pictures may or may not turn out sharp.

○ Dangers of camera shake can be greatly reduced by loading a fast film. If you do not intend to enlarge the pictures to much more than 13x18cm then an ISO 400/27° would be alright. However, if you want larger prints, an ISO 200/24° would be better for general application because of its finer grain but, of course, being slower you will have to be more careful about camera shake. But if the pictures are supposed to be very sharp, e.g., for large prints or slide projection, then I would recommend you use an ISO 100/21° or even slower film. Please also refer to the chapter on films.

○ If the **P** flashes intermittently you should support the camera as firmly as possible, even if it is not blinking at that particular moment, as obviously the lighting conditions are critical.

○ If the display flashes continuously you will have to use a tripod.

○ If it flashes rapidly, then the conditions are altogether unsuitable, as it is too dark to take the shot. The only remedy in this case is to use flash.

○ The opposite is also true and the light could be too strong for even the fastest shutter speed of $\frac{1}{2000}$ sec. and the smallest aperture.

Autofocus Technology

That the Canon EOS cameras focus automatically is not quite as natural as it may sound. It requires a lot of advanced technology – mainly micro electronics. If you are interested in the technological background, then the following pages will be of interest to you. The autofocus technology of the EOS series of cameras is, just like everything else on these cameras, the very best.

In keeping with the best tradition in photographic circles, the introduction of the autofocus facility caused extensive and heated arguments among photographers. And this is how it ought to be. After all, it is only by discussion, criticism and assessment that a new invention

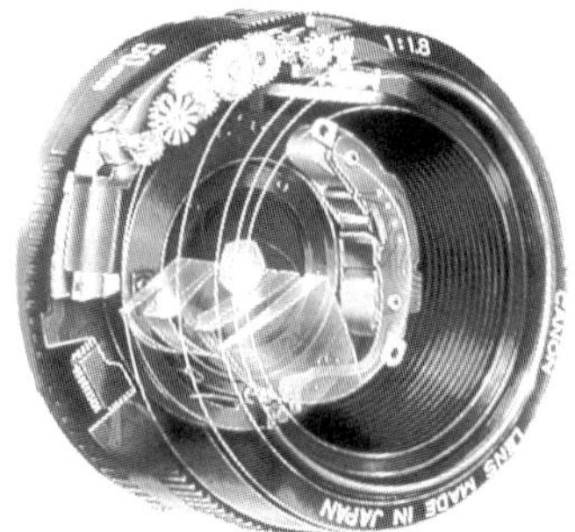

Autofocus requires advanced computer technology in a very restricted space. This view gives an idea of what a modern AF lens contains.

can be properly evaluated and improved to meet requirements. There are many examples in other fields, where the lack of proper thought in the beginning meant that the customer was persuaded to buy something that did not make a lot of sense. Not so with the autofocus facility; this has already proved itself as worthwhile and functional in the short period of its existence. If you still need convincing, perform this little experiment; set the Focus Mode switch on the lens to **M** and set the focusing ring on the lens to infinity; now see how long it takes to focus manually on any subject. Repeat this experiment with the focus set to infinity and the Focus Mode switch to **AF**. The autofocus facility will always be faster than you.

Canon have the most sophisticated technology available – a small, powerful computer that performs a variety of functions. Conversion of analogue to digital signals, querying sensors, driving motors, performing measurements. These data are used in a variety of ways for various control functions. For example some are used to trigger and control the motor to focus the lens. There is also the viewfinder display in the form of the green **P** to indicate danger of camera shake.

This sounds quite simple but consider all the preconditions that are necessary to produce such a warning signal. Firstly, the camera has to be able to ascertain the lens data, because the exposure is controlled by the program mode, which in turn determines which is a suitable aperture/shutter speed combination for the focal length and speed of the attached lens. This information is provided by every Canon EOS System lens in the form of a ROM (Read Only Memory) chip. On request, this provides data to the central processor unit. The data in the ROM are permanently stored there and are retained even if the power supply is disconnected. In the case of zoom lenses the actually selected focal length and maximum aperture (e.g. 28-70mm, f/3.4-4.5) have to be stored via sensors.

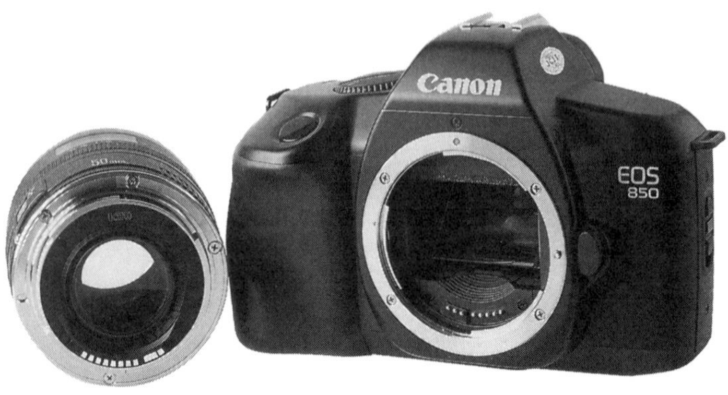

The data transfer between lens and camera is by electronic means, no mechanical elements are necessary.

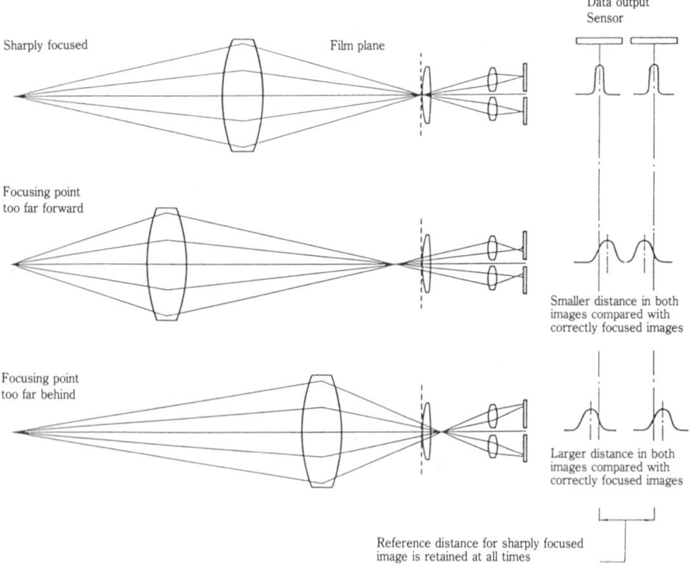

The principle of automatic distance metering. By comparing the image distance with the reference image distance, correct focus is assessed.

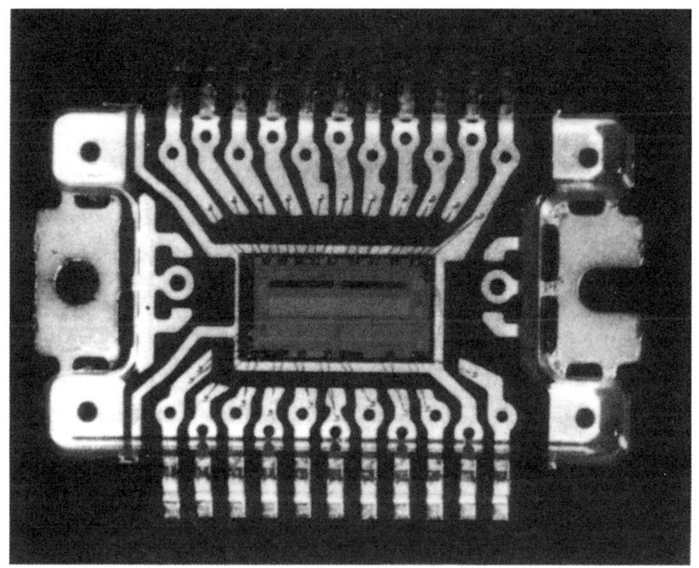

BASIS – the sensor is the heart and brain of the autofocus system. The two sensor areas, responsible for generating the image signals at the centre of the viewfinder, measure only 1.44 x 0.15mm. Amplifier circuits are employed properly to assess the generated signals.

Next, a metering cell in the viewfinder measures the intensity of the light, assessed separately by six sensors, before a final exposure is determined, depending on the speed of the loaded film which is read into the camera computer. Now the central processor can decide whether danger of camera-shake exists by comparing the exposure value with the focal length of the lens. You will remember that the reciprocal of the focal length in mm is the limit for hand-held shutter speeds. After comparing the shutter speed with the focal length of the lens, the processor issues the signal for camera-shake warning or not as the case may be. As you can see, this relatively simple decision is quite a complicated task.

In the above procedure we had not even considered that the EOS is constantly updating all the readings and calculating new values. Every time the release is lightly pressed, the whole process is repeated and all this without even focusing. Just imagine what goes on inside the EOS when you adjust a zoom lens while keeping the release slightly pressed!

Automatic focusing is just as complicated. To be able to perform this function the CPU (Central Processor Unit) requires certain basic information. Here too, the focal length and present focus setting on the lens is ascertained. This information is absolutely necessary to indicate the required amount by which the motors have to adjust the setting of the lens.

TTL-SIR, BASIS and AFD are the technical abbreviations describing the automatic focusing in the Canon EOS cameras. TTL-SIR means metering Through The Lens (TTL) with Secondary Image Registration (SIR). The latter can be explained as the adjustment of two images projected through the lens. In this process, known as phase comparison, two partial images from the autofocus target field are projected onto the line image sensor BASIS (Base Stored Image Sensor). Depending on how closely in focus the subject is, these two images will be offset from each other to a greater or lesser degree. BASIS recognises this analogue signal and converts it into digital information for the processor. The microprocessor, which is in fact a small computer in the EOS, compares this information with its stored reference data and calculates, from the difference between the supplied information and the stored data, the required direction and amount which the motor has to be turned. These data are now used to trigger the AFD (Arc-Form-Drive) in EOS System lenses.

This arc motor is a remarkable invention. Unlike other manufacturers, Canon have been successful in keeping the entire mechanical structure within the lens. Other manufacturers situate a motor in the camera body which drives the lens focusing system. Canon, on the other hand, use

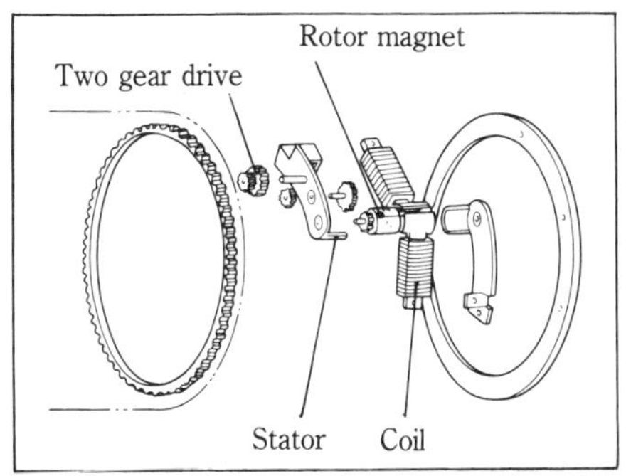
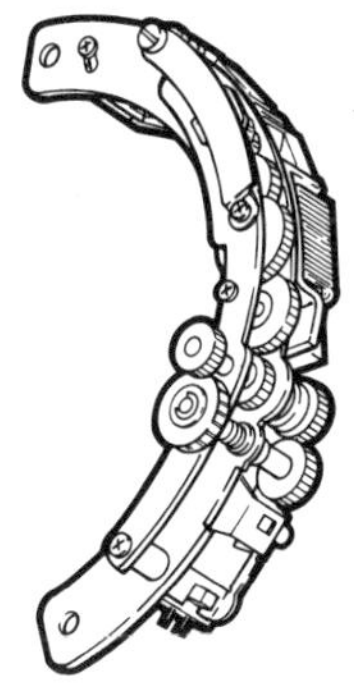

The compactness of the lens is in no way impaired by the unique shape and construction of the arc motor. As the motor is integrated with the lens, the gearing can be exactly designed for the requirements of the particular lens.

two motors built into the lens. One of these is used to adjust the focus, the other the aperture. Their unusual shape is the reason for their name and they were designed this way to fit snugly within the conventional shape of the lens without increasing the overall dimensions. Canon follow the principle of keeping mechanical parts exactly where they are needed.

The main advantage of placing the motor in the lens is firstly that no mechanical couplings are necessary between lens and camera, increasing reliability and speed because only a few mechanical transmissions and short paths are necessary. Furthermore, every motor is optimized for the focusing characteristics of that particular lens and the absence of levers and sprung couplings increase the precision of the control even further.

Apart from the AFD there is another, smaller motor which is responsible for adjusting the aperture. This is the EMD (Electro Magnetic Diaphragm) and is the aperture control in every EOS lens, opening to a tolerance of ⅛ of a stop.

Therefore the bayonet forms the only mechanical connection between camera and lens, all other data are electronically transferred and then converted into the

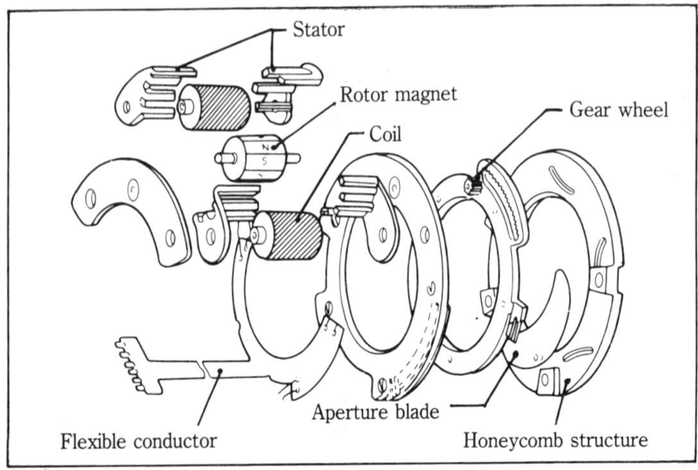

Exploded view of the electromagnetic aperture control EMD.

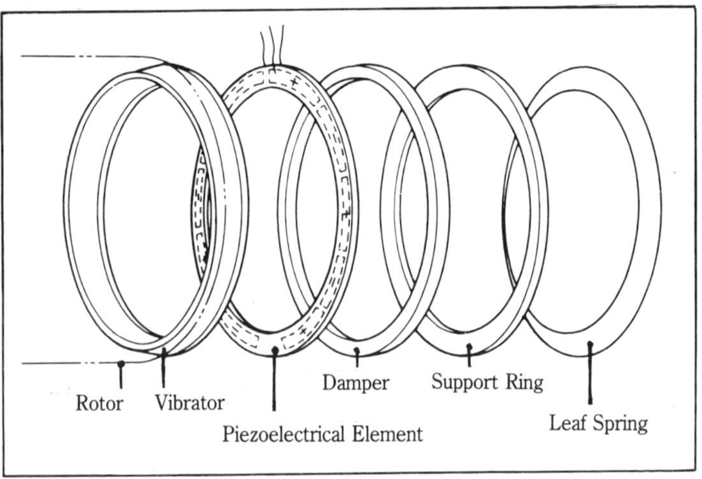

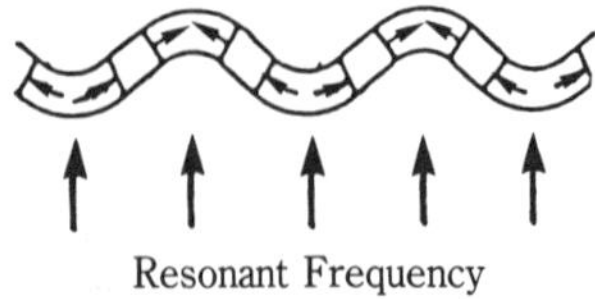

The USM motor is particularly quiet and reliable because of its simple construction.

appropriate actions. This complete separation from the mechanical control brings about direct advantages which are immediately obvious with the special USM (Ultra Sonic Motor) which Canon employs in their fast telephoto lenses; 200mm, f/1.8; 300mm, f/2.8; 600mm, f/4.0. This motor is almost silent and for this reason is particularly sought after by wild-life photographers.

This newly-developed type of motor functions without conventional mechanical elements such as cogs and gears. Its function is therefore quite complicated to explain but nevertheless I shall try; piezoelectric ceramic elements of separate polarities are attached to a ring. A high-frequency alternating current is applied which causes the ceramic elements to expand and contract. This produces a vibration which reverts to a wave motion through the renewed effect of the resonant frequency, after moving through a 90° phase, which in turn drives the motor which moves the focusing unit.

This is all the theory I propose to subject you to. To be quite honest I am not clear how this really works. To help us I shall quote an explanation I have read in one of the magazines: "the USM function is similar to that of a snake — only the other way round. A snake moves by expanding and contracting individual members of its body, this movement manifests itself in waves moving the length of the body. If we hold the snake the floor will move — at least in theory. In the case of the ultrasonic motor this is, in fact, what happens.

The motors and chips integrated in the EOS System are represented in the following tables.

Compared with other autofocus systems the AF technology employed by Canon is different in some respects, although the basic principle is the same. How practical such technology is, regardless of any technical data, becomes quite obvious when we consider the program variation **DEPTH** — the jewel in the crown of any autofocus system. After calculating the closest and the

Microprocessors in the EOS system

Microprocessor	Function
Main microprocessor	control of autofocus, exposure and function sequence
Lens microprocessor	data transfer and EMD/AFD motor control
Speedlite microprocessor	data transfer and zoom reflector control
Technical Back microprocessor	data transfer, data storage and camera function control
Control Motors	
Motor M-1	film transport
Motor M-2	shutter/mirror functions and film rewinding
Motor AFD	lens focusing (arch motor)
Motor USM	lens aperture control (ultrasonic motor)
Motor Zoom	flash reflector-zoom mode (automatic flash angle control)
Shutter magnet (2)	exposure time control

furthest focusing points, the computer decides the most suitable focusing plane and the necessary aperture opening which together will result in the required depth of field.

The working range of the autofocus lies between EV1 and EV18 at ISO 100/21°. This means that the autofocus will work only if the available light is neither too bright nor too dark. For an explanation of the exposure value I will have to lead you a little further into photographic theory. The correct exposure for a subject is controlled by the shutter speed and aperture opening, which in turn depends on the film speed. The lens aperture is the means of controlling the amount of light allowed through the lens at any given time to meet the film. By interaction between the aperture and the speed of the shutter it is possible to

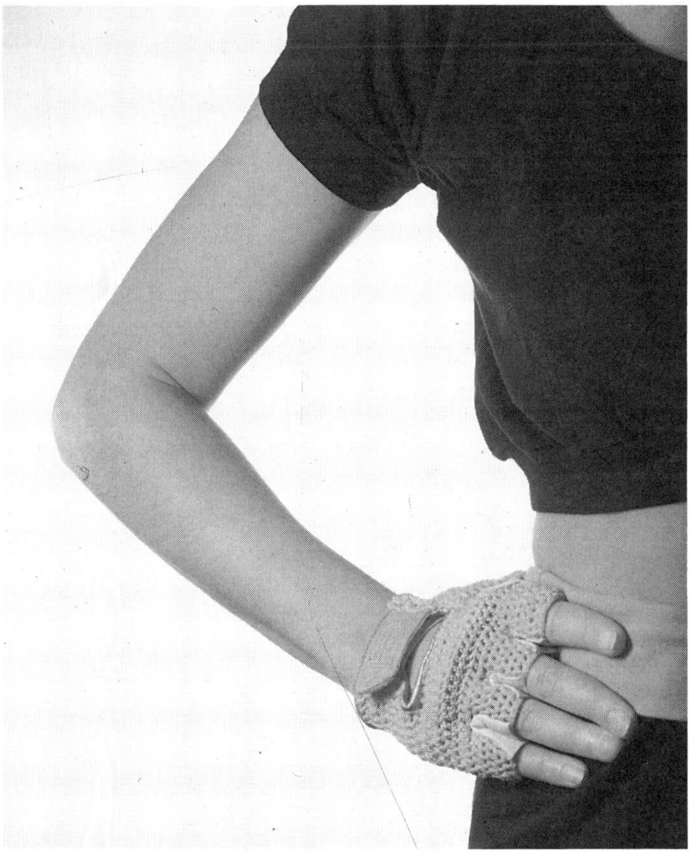

An example of where it is advantageous to deactivate the autofocus. In this photograph the autofocus would have tried to focus on the background as the target field was not aligned with the main subject.

obtain several combinations that will result in the same amount of light exposing the film. If, for example, the amount of light is halved by stopping down the aperture one stop, but simultaneously the shutter exposure time is doubled, then the sum total is the same. Therefore at a certain brightness there are a number of shutter speed/aperture combinations that will result in the correct exposure and this is the exposure value.

All these combinations are assigned a number which is the exposure value for that particular exposure level. An exposure of 1 sec at f/1.4 and all equivalent combinations of exposure times and f/number have an EV of 1. So, 2 secs at f/2, 4 secs at f/2.8, 8 secs at f/4, 16 secs at f/5.6 and so forth, all have an EV of 1. A change of 1 in the EV represents a twofold, one stop, alteration in exposure.

For a better understanding of the limits of the autofocus facility we shall take the example of an exposure value (EV) together with a film speed of ISO 100/21°. EV1 means a shutter speed of 8 secs at aperture f/4. EV18 requires a shutter speed of $\frac{1}{4000}$ sec at the same aperture. As you can see, the working range of the autofocus facility is large and conditions have to become very bright or very dim, before the autofocus cannot function. Apart from the brightness, the subject has to possess a certain contrast for the autofocus facility to work. If the subject is very low in contrast, then the AF facility could fail even if the lighting conditions are greater than EV1.

The shutter speed/aperture combinations do not concern us a great deal when shooting with the EOS 750/850 cameras because the program mode will automatically select suitable combinations. All you need to remember is that the autofocus will not function if the light is exceedingly bright or dim, but this will become apparent after using the camera.

Practical EOS Photography I – Operation

It is a good idea to try out the camera without loading a film. You should be absolutely familiar with all the operating elements and be able to perform the few necessary manipulations in your sleep. It is very simple indeed – switch the EOS on and the rest is done by the camera! But even so, the actual skill lies in proper camera operation. The autofocus seems to go on strike sometimes and then the release will be blocked. How do you get the fast shot on film despite these occasional difficulties?

Tip: first read the handbook from cover to cover and then take a lot of photographs with your new camera. This is very important, especially at the beginning, in order that you become really familiar with it. Don't be too disappointed if some of these pictures fall somewhat short of perfection. On the contrary, one learns best from one's mistakes. From a technical point of view, not much can go wrong, perhaps the occasional incorrect exposure, or even an unsharp picture, if you focused manually. The EOS is a camera with which you can concentrate fully on the subject. But even though the technology of the EOS functions reliably this does not imply that all photographs taken with it will be masterpieces. It is a good policy to be very critical.

Autofocus – The Practical Side

The problem with new technology is that it promises many improvements which often means a period of unfamiliar, sometimes even complicated, handling. The reason is not that the new technology is unsuitable but that our attitudes

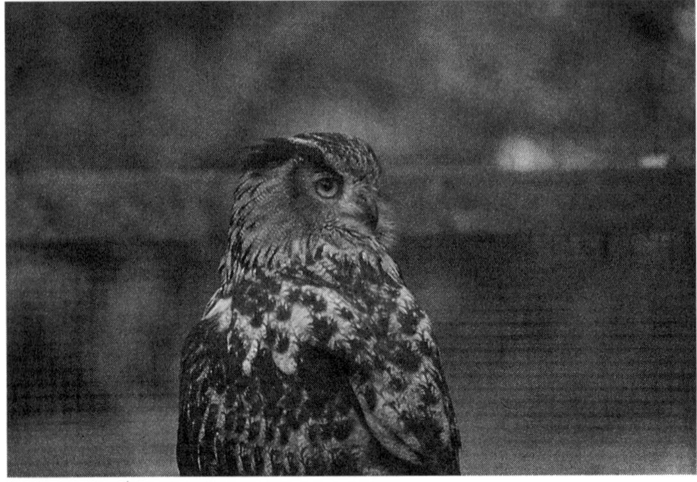

The autofocus is confused by interfering structures between the camera and the subject. It does not know which is the main subject. In this case also the autofocus is better switched off and focusing performed manually. This shot was taken on Agfachrome ISO 1000/31° film, the grain being surprisingly fine for the high speed.

and expectations are still tuned to conventional methods. This is also the case when first using autofocus.

Everything tends to work well the first time you use the autofocus facility. The main subject is brought into the centre of the frame, it is well-lit and possesses adequate contrast. But the next time you want to place the subject more towards the edge of the frame, or, perhaps, the subject is in a dark corner, or the autofocus just cannot focus on the chosen subject, nothing seems to work. Then we are most annoyed with all this useless technology. This is a shame because a little forethought and know-how can solve any problem. I shall endeavour to help with the

---

Sports events are a source of great excitement for any photographer. Suitable scenes present themselves in abundance. The program mode of the EOS will take care of all exposure settings. Still, take a few spare rolls of film, because whenever you are dealing with fast action it is difficult to assess whether or not a picture will be satisfactory.

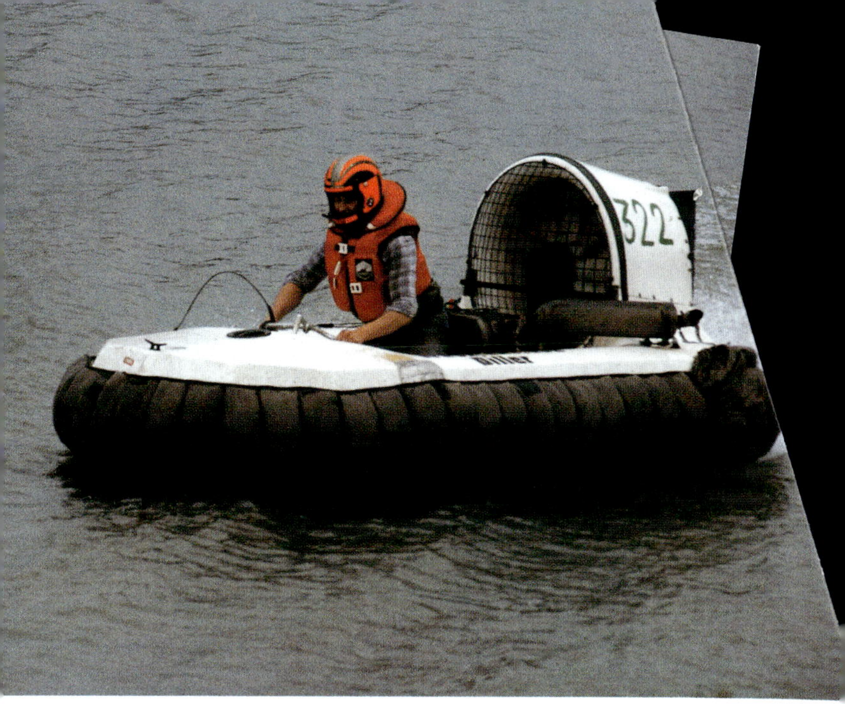

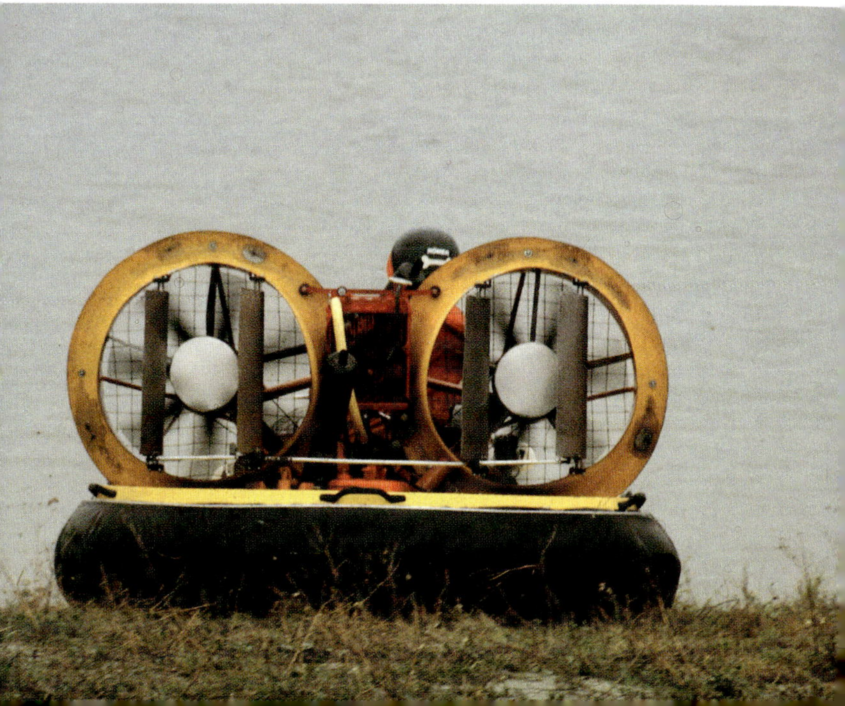

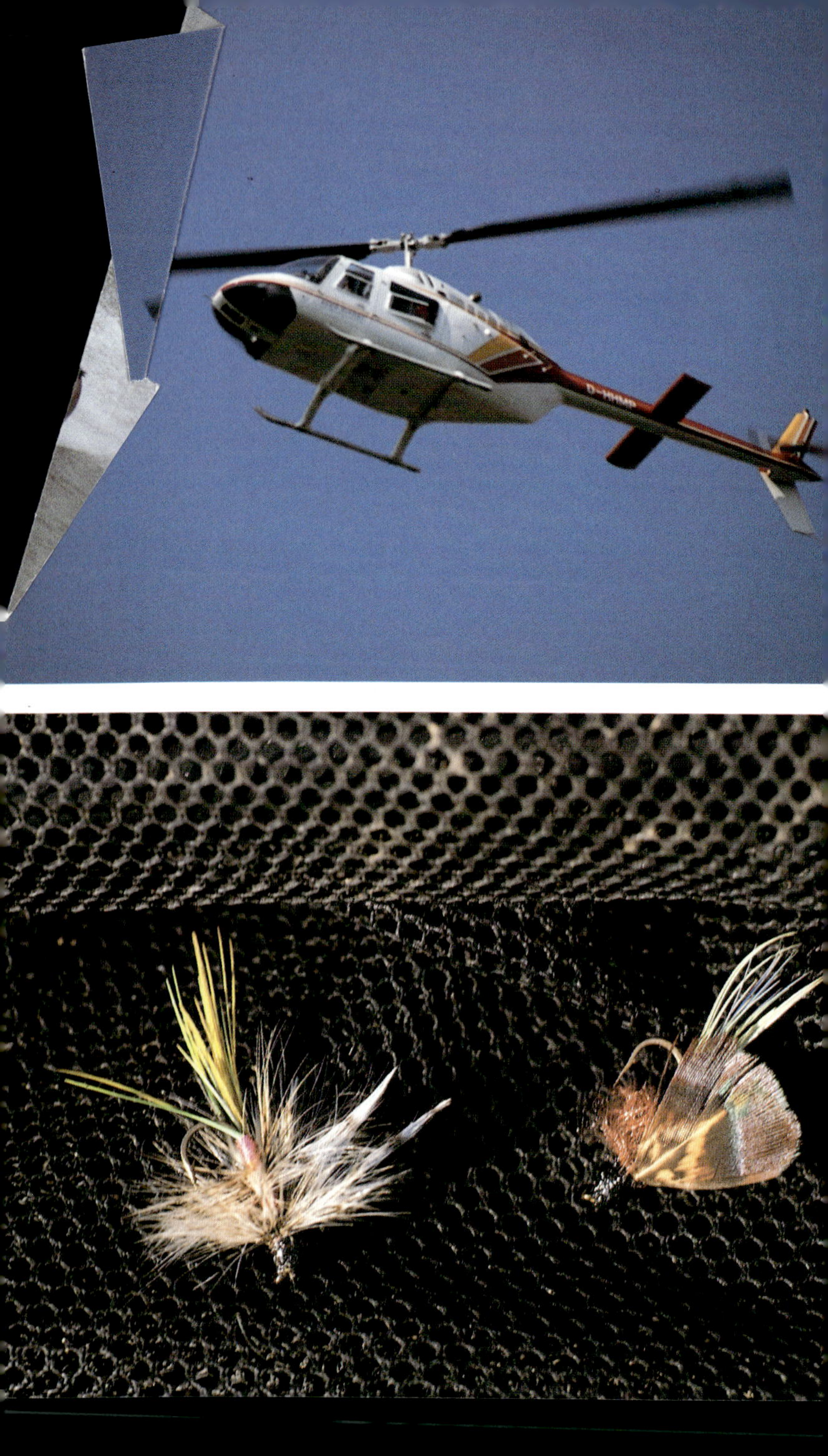

know-how. Then I would recommend that you use the autofocus in a variety of situations to get the feel of it. Do try and look for difficult situations and see how these can be dealt with.

The possibilities and limitations of this new technology are best discovered by exploration and soon you will understand the conditions that present problems to the autofocus. Better still, you will be able to understand the difficulty and be able to analyse it, forestall it and find the best way to overcome it. The frustrating moments when the autofocus does fail and you have missed a good shot will be few and far between as you master this facility.

At the centre of the viewfinder is the autofocus target field which is crucial in any attempt to find the correct focus. Two partial images are sent from this small metering field to the sensor BASIS, and these data in turn are used by the microprocessor for assessing the sharpness. This small field must be made to coincide with a subject detail that the autofocus finds acceptable for focusing. The criteria for a suitable focusing area are as follows:

○ the subject in the focusing field must not be too brightly illuminated (nearly an academic situation as an EV value of 18 can rarely be exceeded)
○ the subject must not be too dark
○ the subject must have sufficient contrast and detail (the autofocus cannot focus on a smooth wall)
○ no confusing elements should be in the metering field

These two examples demonstrate the application of both automatic modes.

Top: The program mode of the EOS will automatically select fast shutter speeds in bright conditions. The fast shutter speed of ¹/₂₀₀₀ sec., when shooting into a bright sky, almost freezes the fast movement of the helicopter's rotor.

Bottom: The depth mode was used here to ensure that the angler's flies were focused sharply.

such as a fence with equally-spaced uprights
○ the subject should not move too fast

Luckily, there are solutions for all the above difficulties. First, the most improbable complication − too bright. This is indeed most unlikely as EV18 corresponds to an aperture of f/22 and a shutter speed of $\frac{1}{500}$ sec., or another equivalent combination. Such values are found if you are photographing directly into the sun for example. If this situation does arise, then there are two possible solutions; change to manual focusing or attach a neutral density filter to the lens. Such neutral density (ND) filters are available in various depths and work like sunglasses − the autofocus is no longer blinded and functions properly.

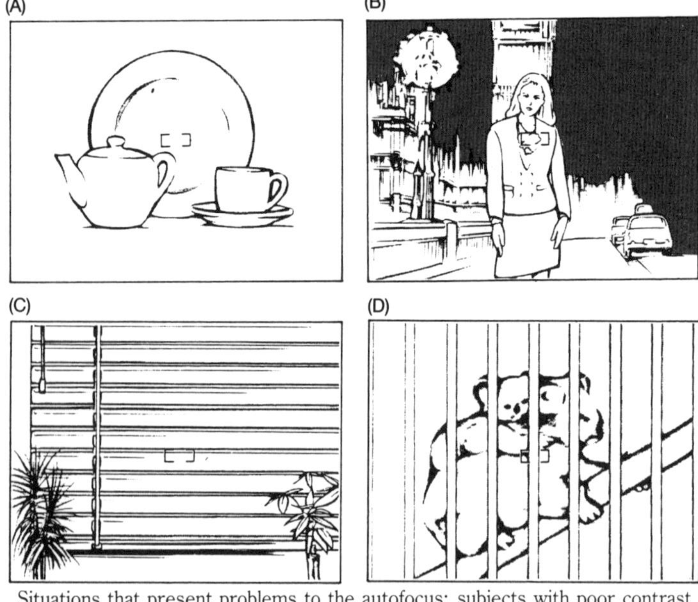

Situations that present problems to the autofocus: subjects with poor contrast (A), low lighting conditions (B), horizontal structures (C), and confusing details in the foreground (D). In two instances (C & D) it will suffice to turn or incline the camera slightly to find a more suitable subject area for focusing. The focus setting is stored by keeping the release lightly pressed, so that the camera can be re-aligned for the desired framing. In all four cases manual focusing will produce satisfactory results.

Such filters are useful if you are holidaying in the tropics and wish to photograph mermaids on a white sandy beach!

In extremely poor light you could have to resort to manual focusing. The use of a flashgun is another possibility and will allow the autofocus to function even in total darkness for subjects up to 6m away. The flashgun will project an infrared metering pattern onto the subject which the autofocus will use to focus.

This metering flash could also assist you if the subject is a large smooth surface with little contrast. But flash illumination is not always desirable and the other alternative would again be manual focusing. In most situations it will suffice, though, to simply move the camera a little either way to bring a different subject area within the target field. To find a suitable detail look out for edges. Press the release lightly to focus, keep it pressed, and re-align the camera to the original position. The same also applies if a confusing detail obscures the main subject in the target field.

To capture fast subjects (racing vehicles, insects, etc.), there are two methods. Either focus on a substitute focusing point (at the same distance as the anticipated event) in advance, keep the release lightly pressed, and wait until the subject moves into the desired position before fully pressing the shutter release button. This will not always be the best method. You will have to ensure that the substitute focusing point is comparable in its exposure value to that of the actual subject, because both the focus and the exposure value are stored simultaneously. In some cases it will be more practical to focus manually. For subjects further than 2 metres from the camera, the focusing point can be preselected and the release effected when the subject moves into sharp focus. For smaller shooting distances it may be better to select a shooting distance and then move the camera closer/ further away from the subject until it appears sharp on the focusing screen.

Tips/conclusion: Divide the preparations for a particular shot into individual steps. The automatic focusing and selection of subject framing should be treated separately. Otherwise you are always likely to produce pictures where the main subject is in exactly the centre of the frame and this can be rather boring. You proceed as follows:

○ point at the main subject and press release lightly. The camera will automatically focus and retain the setting.
○ The exposure value is retained at the same time. This implies an additional advantage; the exposure will be exactly right for the point where the main subject is situated.
○ Now the camera may be realigned for the desired framing and the release fully pressed.
○ Keeping the release pressed, the focusing and exposure are measured again and another picture is taken.

The above procedure sounds more complicated than it really is. The time taken to re-align the camera need not be more than a fraction of a second. By keeping the two functions — focusing and shutter release — strictly separate, they can nevertheless be combined into a single movement; point — lightly press release — re-align camera — press release fully.

Tip 1: Don't worry if the autofocus goes on strike. Try another, equally distant point nearby or tilt the camera slightly, this helps in the majority of cases.
Tip 2: Having tried everything else and the autofocus is still unable to find a focusing point, change over to manual focusing.
Tip 3: The front element and filter thread of some EOS lenses rotate during focusing. Some filters (polarising filter, starburst filter) need to be in a certain position for maximum effect. In this case it would

be better to focus manually and check the correct position of the filter. This prevents the autofocus adjusting the focusing point which might cancel the intended effect of the filter.

Clever Multi-field Metering

The basic requirement for the success of every program mode, however sophisticated, is a reliable exposure metering system. After all, the program mode can only assign a combination of aperture value/shutter speed to the exposure value ascertained by the metering system. The program mode does not change the exposure in any way, it simply converts it. The amount of light allowed to expose the film is not changed.

If the underlying exposure metering is incorrect even the most sophisticated program mode will not be able to produce a correctly exposed picture. To produce pictures that are exposed as correctly as possible, Canon have introduced a system of multi-field metering whereby the viewfinder image is divided into six individual segments, as shown in the diagram. The centre of the picture is heavily weighted, compared with the outer regions, because, as you already know, the exposure value is stored together with the focusing point. As the autofocus target field is also located at the centre of the screen, this method ensures that the main subject is properly considered when determining the exposure.

Based on the results of measuring the individual fields the electronics perform a contrast evaluation and compare this with internally stored data. This analysis is performed to ascertain whether the given subject possesses particularly high contrast, whether it might be a backlit shot, whether fill-in flash is necessary, or whether the illumination is insufficient so as to require flash, etc. Then a suitable aperture/shutter speed combination is determined and, if appropriate, the attached/integrated flash is trig-

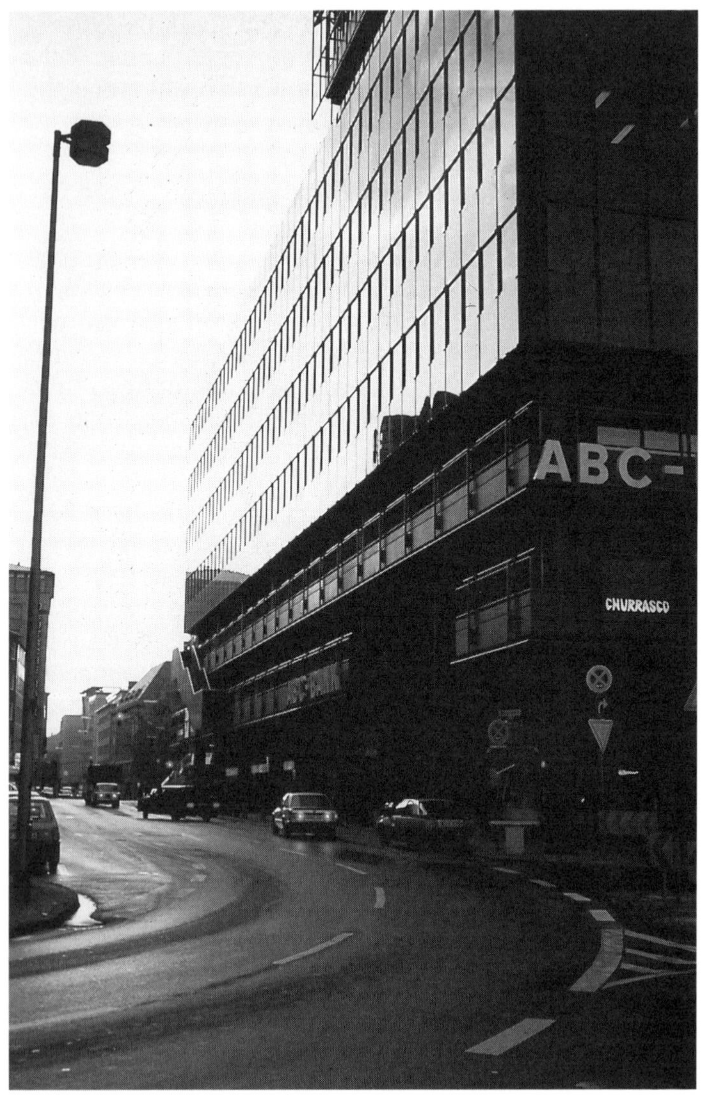

The multi-field metering system of the EOS masters even difficult lighting conditions like this with high contrast and uneven brightness distribution.

The brightness of the viewfinder image is assessed in six different fields with the centre of the frame heavily weighted. Focus setting and exposure are measured and stored by lightly pressing the release. As the centre of the picture contributes more than the rest, the metering results can be influenced by changing the focusing area.

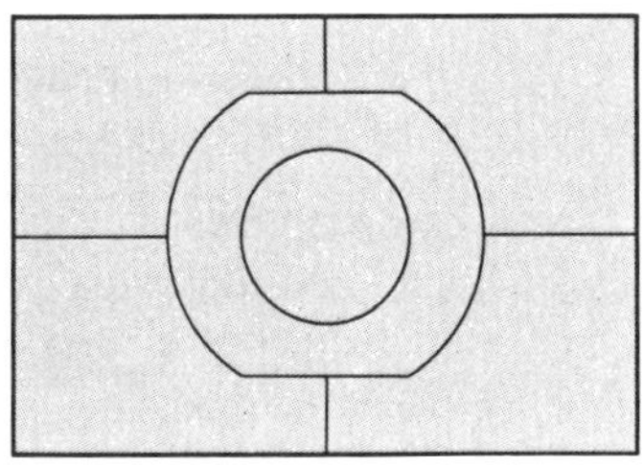

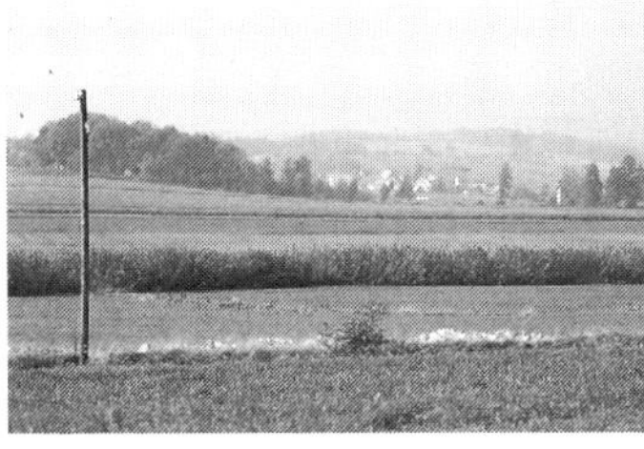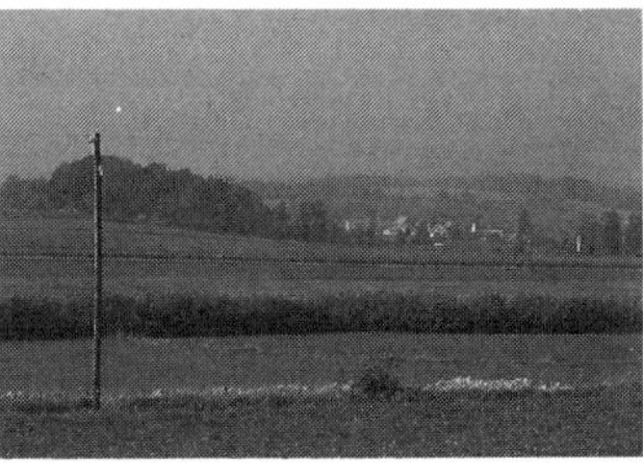

The foreground was chosen as a metering area in the brighter picture and the EOS assesses the scene as rather dark and overexposes to compensate. In the darker picture, when the sky was used as a metering area, the EOS assesses the scene as rather bright and underexposes. After the metering value is stored the release is kept pressed and the camera is re-aligned for the desired framing.

gered for subject illumination or fill-in flash. Multi-field metering is very reliable and there are hardly any lighting situations that the EOS system cannot cope with.

In this field too, modern technology has proved its worth by translating many years experience of countless photographers into electronic impulses. This is similar to the camera-shake warnings provided by the EOS, which are controlled in relation to the selected focal length and which were technically more difficult to realize. When introduced, electronic exposure metering only performed metering tasks which were then presented to the photographer to decide how the measured value had to be interpreted for a given subject and lighting condition. This assessment is now also performed by the EOS and the photographer can leave this, sometimes difficult task, to the electronic brain in his camera. He can be assured that

51

all necessary factors are taken into account and that generally speaking he could not have done it any better.

Tips/Conclusion:
○ Focusing and exposure metering are coupled. The area of the focusing target field is strongly weighted in exposure metering.
○ The viewfinder area is divided into six segments and analysed to obtain as precise and suitable an exposure as possible. This system performs well in difficult situations.

Controlled Program Mode

As the EOS models 750 and 850 do not provide any information as to which aperture and shutter speed are chosen for what situation, it is not a bad idea to examine the program curve. This is not quite as simple to interpret, but I shall endeavour to explain it for you to be able to appreciate what the camera is doing, when and why. Under certain circumstances the EOS is programmed to perform specific assessments and your knowledge of how this has been arranged should improve the quality of your pictures.

In the early days of photography the photographer had to perform all assessments and settings on the camera himself. The first step towards easy camera handling was a built-in exposure meter, which measured the brightness of the subject. Aperture and shutter speed were then adjusted manually, until two pointers were aligned, to achieve correct exposure. The next development was cameras on which the photographer selected a suitable aperture value and the camera automatically selected and set a suitable shutter speed − aperture priority was born! Later the aperture too could be automatically controlled for a preselected shutter speed. On cameras with shutter

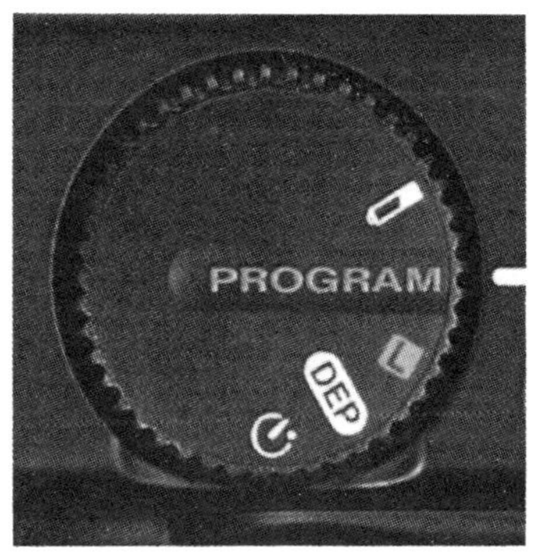

Instead of tele, wide-angle or normal program mode; the main switch is set to **PROGRAM**. The camera's computer reads the focal length of the lens fitted and selects the appropriate program curve.

speed priority or aperture priority mode the photographer has to preselect either the shutter speed or the aperture. Cameras with program mode will perform both settings automatically. This is not done arbitrarily, of course, but according to the subject brightness and film speed, producing a certain exposure value which is then converted into an appropriate aperture/shutter speed combination.

The first program mode cameras were relatively simple. The second generation of automatic cameras offered a variety of programs and priority modes. There were telephoto and wide-angle program modes in addition to the normal program mode. By selecting the appropriate program variation the exposure could be influenced to favour faster shutter speeds for longer focal lengths to avoid camera-shake and smaller aperture openings for wide-angle lenses to obtain a large depth of field. This arrangement extended automatic facilities to a considerable degree.

But the owner of an EOS camera need not worry about anything; all he needs to do is set the Selector Dial to **Program**, the rest is done by the camera. Dependent on the speed and focal length of the attached lens the camera automatically selects the correct program. First let's look at the program curve for the EF 50mm, f/1.8 lens. Tracing the line from left to right you will note that it follows a

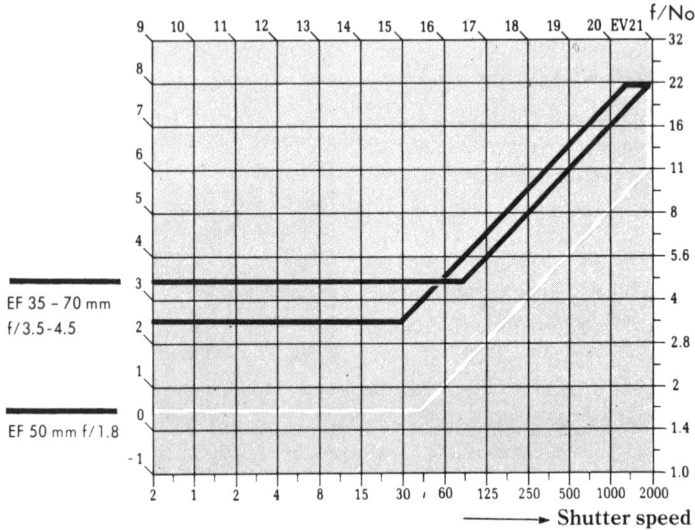

According to which program curve has been selected, the EOS sets the shutter speed and aperture.

straight line up to a shutter speed of ¼₅ sec. The aperture is kept constant at the widest opening of f/1.8. This means as long as the lighting conditions are poor the aperture is kept fully open and only the shutter speed is varied. Only when the subject gets brighter are both aperture value and shutter speed altered. The aperture is stopped down and the shutter speed is increased in steps. As you can see, this continues down to an exposure value equal to an aperture of f/11 and a shutter speed of ½₀₀₀ sec. The conditions are very bright now and the fastest shutter speed has been utilized; only the aperture can still be stopped down in case it gets even brighter.

To summarize, the following picture emerges, which applies to every type of lens; the EOS is programmed to keep the aperture at its maximum until the shutter speed is fast enough to minimise the risk of camera-shake. From that point onwards, both aperture and shutter speed are adjusted, step-by-step, until the fastest available shutter speed is attained. If the subject brightness is greater than that, then the aperture is stopped down even further. You can check this by examining the two upper graph lines for the EF 35-70mm, f/3.5-4.5 Zoom lens. The program curve behaves differently depending on the focal length selected on the lens. The curve makes a change in direction only after the shutter speed reaches a value equal to 1/focal length of the attached lens.

The special feature of this facility; the program graph line of the EOS is arranged so that it is dependent on the speed and focal length of the attached lens. This ensures that the automatic facility of the EOS chooses, in every situation, a reasonable combination of shutter speed and aperture, preventing camera-shake to a large degree on the one hand, and ensuring sufficient depth of field on the other, if lighting conditions allow. If you do not like the way the program mode controls the settings, you can always override them. The aperture (to be more precise, the depth of field) can be easily controlled. This will be explained later. The shutter speed, on the other hand, can only be indirectly controlled via film speed or the DEPTH program. A fast film requires less exposure and this therefore allows faster shutter speeds. Setting rather narrow limits for the depth of field in the **DEPTH** mode will select large apertures and therefore fast shutter speeds.

Tips/Conclusion:
○ The program mode is dependent on the focal length
○ The program curve keeps the aperture fully open until a safe shutter speed has been obtained: 1/focal length is sufficient (+/− half a stop)
○ This is how the critical shutter speeds are exceeded most quickly
○ Aperture and shutter speed are then adjusted by equal increments to obtain the best possible compromise of aperture and shutter speed.

Depth Program

DEPTH is a program variation that demonstrates clearly how technical progress can bring about real improvements. Most camera manufacturers did away with aperture stop-down buttons in the process of making their cameras automatic. This development has not been universally welcomed. The stop-down button was an important facility for the photographer to check on the viewfinder screen how far the depth of field extended for the given aperture. He could assess whether his subject was in sharp focus from front to back. This assessment by viewfinder screen was rather difficult, especially as the image becomes increasingly darker the smaller the aperture became. However, it is better to have this facility than not at all.

This omission has been overcome by an almost revolutionary facility. In the program variation **DEPTH** you only need to point the camera at the closest and then the furthest focusing point, between which the subject is supposed to be in sharp focus, the camera's electronics will do the rest. It determines the actual depth of the subject space, calculates the appropriate aperture and the best focusing distance. Do not worry if the EOS, after determining the depth of field, focuses the lens at an apparently wrong focusing plane and the image does not

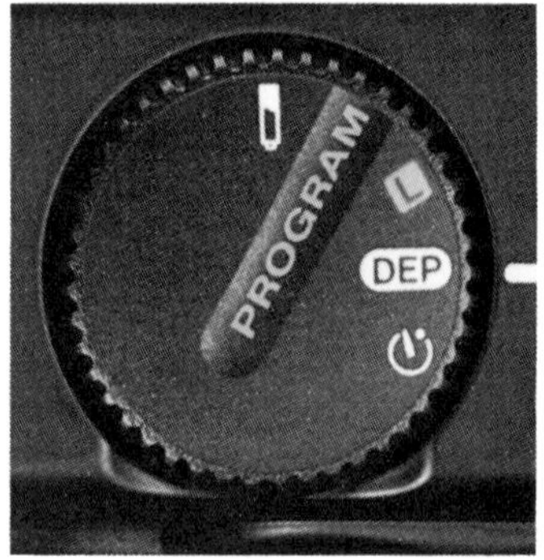

The program variation **DEPTH** is activated by the selector dial. This is doubtless the most useful development since autofocus.

appear sharp in the viewfinder. You may rely on the camera's judgment to choose the best possible focusing plane with smallest possible aperture to sharply depict the subject within the range which you specified.

By stopping down the aperture less light is allowed to expose the film. This has the advantage of increasing the depth of field. On the other hand, because less light is allowed to enter, the shutter speed has to be slowed. For this reason the green **P** may blink in the viewfinder, warning you of danger of camera-shake, although the **P** did not blink when shooting the same subject in normal program mode.

You will have to accept that however good this facility is, it cannot transgress physical laws. Impossible situations do not become more probable, however excellent the technical facilities. Depth of field from the tip of the nose to infinity is a tall order, even for the EOS. You will therefore have to determine reasonable limits for your depth of field and a shorter focal length lens, to obtain reasonable spatial depth.

On the other hand, when using this mode you may wish

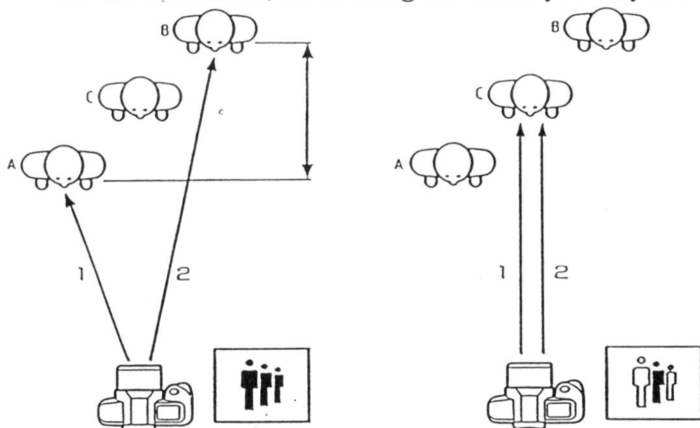

In the **DEPTH** mode, depth of field can be determined by measuring first the closest point to the camera and then the farthest, between which the subject is supposed to be shown in sharp focus. It is also possible to ensure narrow depth of field by measuring two points close to each other.

to limit the depth of field to emphasise the main subject against a blurred background. This will be subject to physical limitations as well. A 24mm wide-angle lens has a relatively large depth of field, even with fully open aperture. To keep the depth of field small, you will therefore have to reach for a longer focal length lens.

Tips/Conclusion:
○ To use the **DEPTH** program variation; focus first on the closer focusing point and press the release button lightly.
○ Take your finger off the release button, point at the furthest focusing point and repeat focusing procedure.
○ Take your finger off the release button, realign camera for the desired framing and lightly press the release button again. The camera will now calculate the necessary exposure and aperture settings. Now you can fully release the shutter.
○ Try to limit the depth of field as precisely as possible. After all, this is the whole point of providing this mode. To choose larger than actually-desired limits will have negative effects. To obtain the largest depth of field the aperture will have to be stopped down even further and the shutter speed will become excessively slow.
○ Take particular note of the green **P** in the viewfinder. If it flashes you should look for some sort of support, a tripod being ideal.
○ Do not forget: this mode may be used to obtain as large or as small a depth of field as possible.
○ Wide-angle lenses produce larger depths of field
○ Telephoto lenses produce narrower depths of field.

Intelligent Program Mode

It might seem that the program mode is the best thing for photography since the proverbial introduction of sliced bread. However, there are good reasons why some cameras have, apart from the program mode, other exposure modes such as shutter speed priority, aperture priority, or even fully manual. EOS offer the 620 and the 650 cameras as excellent examples. The EOS 750 and 850 cameras determine the exposure values for the photographer, the 620 and 650 models, on the other hand, allow the photographer to preset certain parameters in line with individual photographic intentions. These remarks should not put you off your EOS 750/850 — on the contrary. Enjoy the easy and trouble-free operation, the way your camera performs all the tricky calculations, leaving you free to concentrate on your subject. However, if you find after gaining experience that certain questions keep on bothering you, then you may be ready for the next step. Thoughts such as "I wish I could set aperture f/5.6 now", or "a correction factor of $-\frac{1}{2}$ stop would be in order", or "a shutter speed of $\frac{1}{500}$ sec. would be best in this situation" are a clear indication that you should think of buying a camera with more facilities.

If you are one of those photographers who can't be bothered thinking too hard about the technical facilities; who is entirely happy with the way the camera handles and the final pictures, then this does not mean that you are not a discerning photographer. All it means is that you have chosen the right instrument for your purposes — and the EOS 750/850 are amongst the best.

Energy Supply

Don't allow yourself to be confused by questions such as "what is the mechanical shutter speed of your EOS?". This trick question is supposed to reveal that your EOS will not work without batteries. Well — so what?

After the introduction of the integrated exposure meter, manufacturers soon changed over to electronic control of the shutter as well. This was done for a good reason.

Electronic shutter speed control is far more precise than any mechanical device could ever be. However, old-fashioned photographers found it annoying to have to think about carrying spare batteries. Regardless of the advantages of automatic exposure metering and precise control of the shutter speed, mechanical shutter speed control was clamoured for, and the manufacturers obliged to satisfy the popular demand.

EOS cameras depend even more on battery power than previous generation cameras. For example, film transport and aperture control are electronically controlled. Therefore: no batteries — no pictures! This is no real disadvantage. To be able to use a single-speed, mechanically-controlled, shutter when nothing else, in particular the exposure metering, is functioning, is of doubtful use. Nobody would seriously consider pushing a motor car just because the battery is flat. Other remedies are called for. The remedy against embarrassing break-downs is quite simple — a spare battery. This solution is by far the better one and everything will work perfectly — so why bother with mechanical shutter operation?

The EOS uses a single battery for all its functions. It supplies energy for all the microprocessors and drives the motors in the camera and lens. Only a lithium battery 2CR5 is suitable. The capacity of this battery will be sufficient for 75 films in the EOS 850 and for about 40 films in the 750 models. This figure allows for the use of flash with 30% of the pictures. With average use the photographer will probably have to replace the battery once a year which is quite reasonable.

Tip: Always carry a spare battery. Store it in the fridge or even freezer to prevent spontaneous discharge. It will be as good as new when you have to use it.

Cleaning and Care of Your Camera

There isn't a lot that you have to remember. The most important thing is always to replace the various covers on the lens and camera body. Never leave the camera or a lens unprotected. This prevents the front or rear elements on the lens or the mirror in the camera becoming scratched or marked.

As there is usually a lens attached to the camera, the bayonets are well protected and need no special cleaning.

If you always take care and attach the protective covers, the only part of the camera that will need regular cleaning is the front element of the lens. Whether the exterior of the camera lens is kept clean is more a question of personal standards than necessity. It should suffice wiping the exterior now and then with a soft cloth.

On the other hand, dirt on the front element is detrimental to the picture quality. What's more, lenses seem to exert a magnetic attraction on dust. This leads to the danger that if you are particularly addicted to cleanliness you could easily overdo it! This too would be totally wrong. It is preferable to leave a little dust on the front element, rather than try to remove every speck by thorough rubbing. The delicate front element is only too easily damaged, every little grain of dust acts as an abrasive, scratching the delicate surface. I would therefore recommend the following three steps for cleaning:

○ Use a dusting brush to clean the front element, pressurized air is best. Blowing or breathing on the lens could leave little droplets of saliva on the lens which can be harmful.

○ Remove fingermarks and other stains carefully with lens cleaning tissues

○ If there are still some marks left, remove these by careful circular movements. Always think about the abrasive effect of dust.

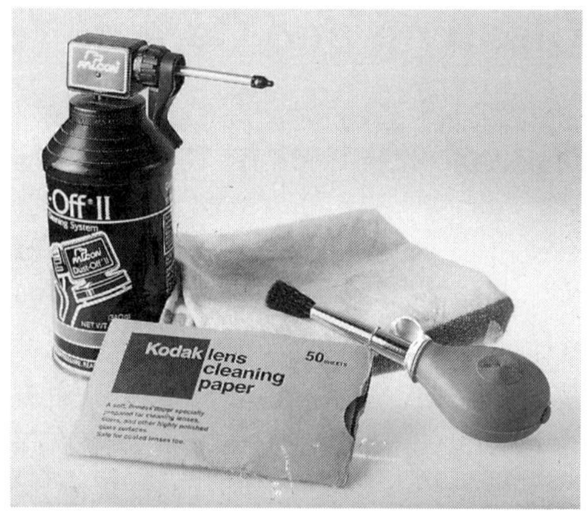

A simple cleaning set, easily assembled, to keep your entire set of equipment clean.

Personally I think special lens cleaning tissue is better than a lens cloth. Paper is used once only and then thrown away – even if it is still clean. A cloth, on the other hand, is used over a period of time during which plenty of dirt and dust have a chance to accumulate.

This should be enough. Only in very stubborn cases will you have to think about a good general clean. Proceed, as outlined above, in the above order, finally wiping off any fingermarks, etc.

To avoid most problems of keeping the front element clean, many photographers permanently attach a UV or skylight filter to it. These types of filters are reasonably priced, protect the front element against scratches, rain, etc. and are easily replaced. Theoretically they are supposed to reduce the reproduction quality but with a good multi-coated lens they will not have any adverse effects on your picture quality. I doubt whether you would be able to discern any quality difference between pictures taken with and those without a UV filter.

Lenses – The Means to Image Creation

Canon has always been in the forefront as far as a good selection of lenses is concerned. Before the introduction of the EOS system, this may not have been self-evident; it was because camera models used to change over the years but not the bayonets. The introduction of a new camera did not necessitate any new lenses. All this changed with the advent of the EOS cameras. The new technology necessitated a new bayonet and therefore a range of new EOS lenses. It is not enough to buy a new EOS body, to avail yourself of the new autofocus technology, you will also have to buy new lenses. Some Canon photographers may bemoan this fact. However, all those who did decide on the purchase of an EOS system came to appreciate the advantages, because the necessity of developing a new lens system meant that the latest technological advances could be incorporated in their construction.

Optical Correction

The endeavour to construct lenses that are corrected to the highest possible degree necessitates the use of several elements, arranged in groups, whereby different types of glass and element shapes are incorporated. Terms such as chromatic aberration, spherical aberration, coma, astigmatism, curvature of field, distortion and vignetting are all possible errors, presenting the optical engineers with real challenges. Differently shaped lenses and types of glasses are combined to achieve a total of zero errors. The 100% error-free lens does not exist, it is an impossibility because of physical laws, but you may be

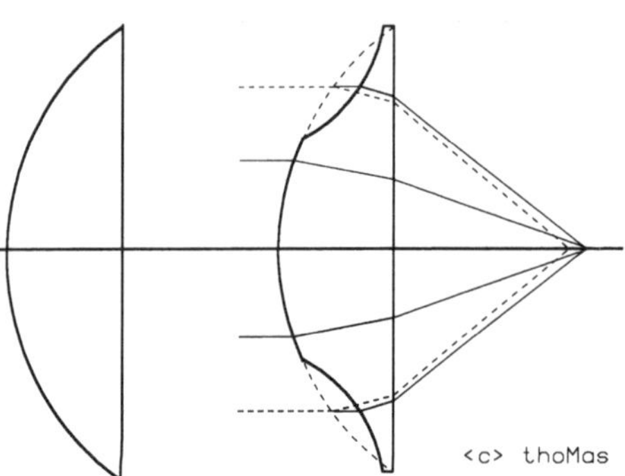

Unlike conventional lenses (left), aspherical lenses (right) possess more than one curvature. This ensures that even the rays from the edge of the lens are refracted to the same focus. The dotted line shows the focus for conventional lenses.

assured that all Canon EOS lenses are corrected to a very high degree and as such may be used in almost any situation.

One decisive step towards fast, compact, and highly-corrected lenses was the introduction of the aspherical lens. Contrary to conventional lenses, where the cross-section is always an arc of a circle, aspherical lenses have several curvatures. Obviously, these are more difficult to produce and the manufacturing methods have so far been rather cumbersome and expensive. For this reason aspherical elements were used only in the more expensive lenses. Meantime Canon have managed to develop a special production method so that these new elements are now efficiently employed, at a reasonable price, in their EF range.

The advantage of using aspherical elements is not only the better correction of reproduction errors, in particular spherical aberration. In conventional lenses the rays at the edge are refracted differently from those at the centre, the result being several focal points — the so-called spherical aberration. In conventional lenses this error is corrected to a large extent by combining several diverging

---

Night shots have their own particular charm but you will need a very fast film and a tripod. A tripod was used for the top picture. In the bottom picture the exceedingly fast Ektachrome P 800/1600 did the job.

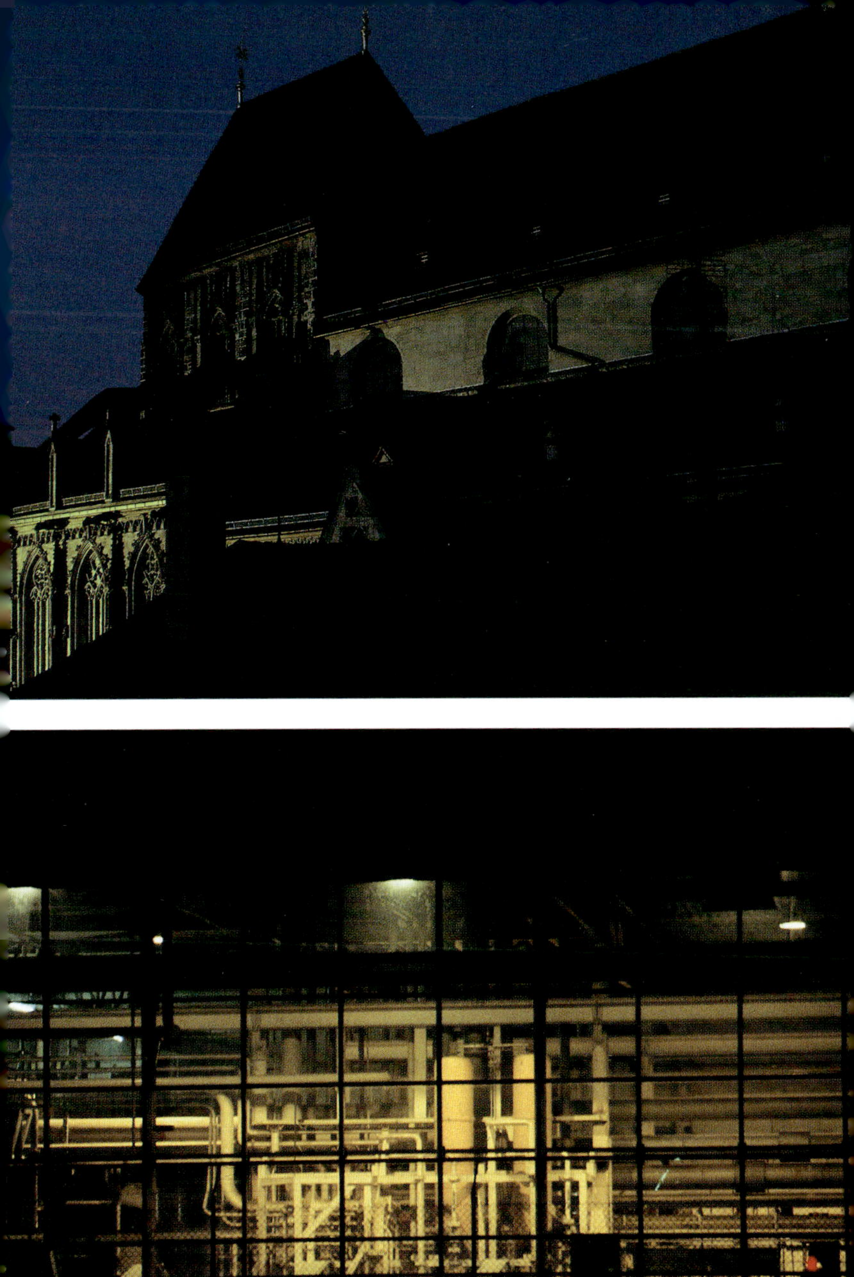

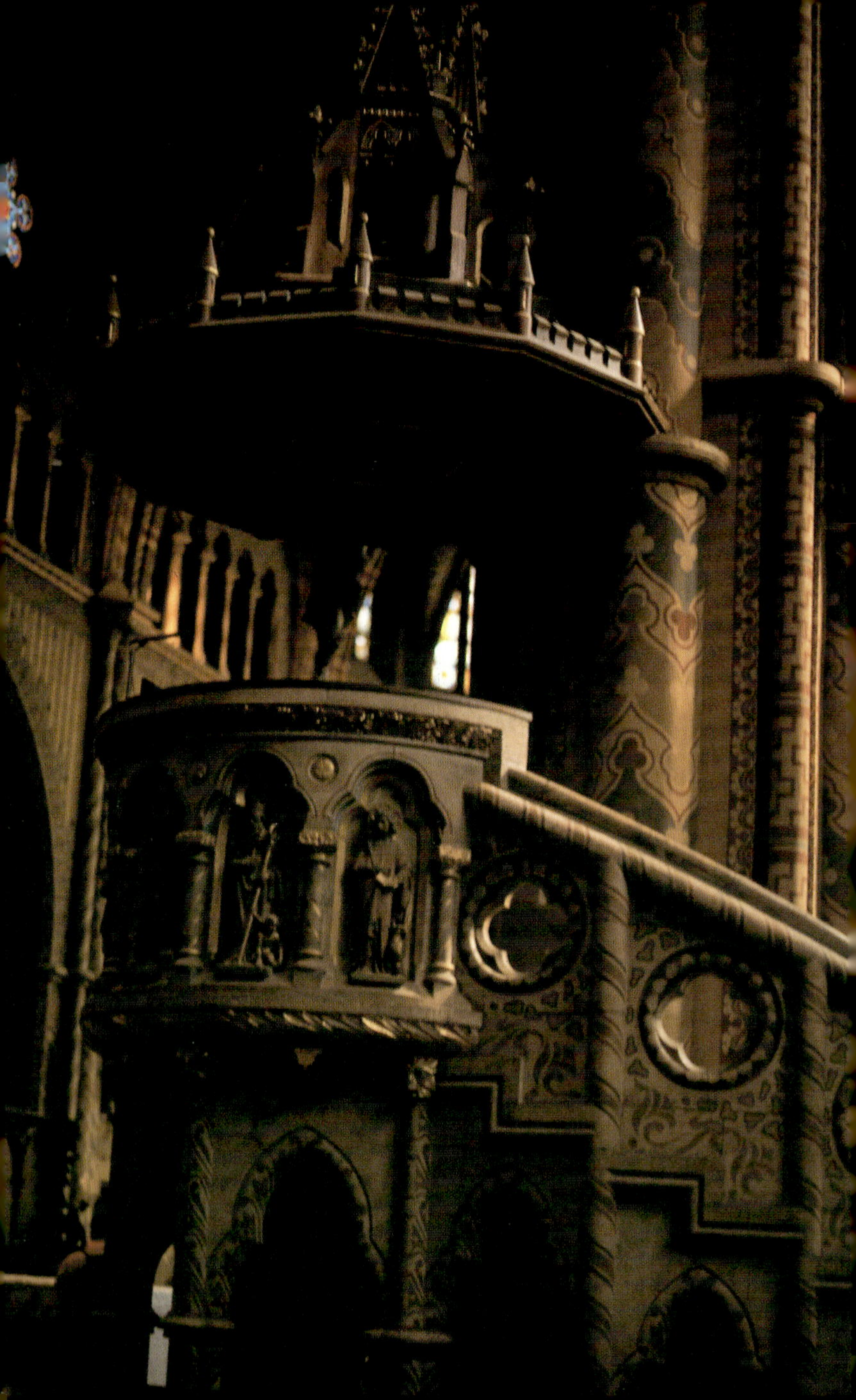

and converging elements. Stopping down the aperture is also very helpful in reducing this unwanted effect as this reduces the relative quantity of marginal rays. Aspherical lenses can be produced so that a single element will produce a single focal point across the entire surface of the element. This is particularly favourable in the construction of zoom lenses, because in this way the aberration may be corrected throughout its entire focal length range. In the construction of exceedingly fast lenses with high reproduction quality at fully open aperture the aspherical elements are also indispensable. Last but not least, the inclusion of these types of lenses makes the overall construction much more compact and lighter, because fewer elements are used in the overall construction. The new production method allows the inclusion of these otherwise very expensive elements in their EOS lenses and most of the range includes one or more.

I am sure that I am not overstating the case when I say that aspherical lenses herald a new golden age in photography. For equal or better reproduction quality, lenses in future will be lighter and smaller. A zoom lens covering fixed focal lengths from 28 to 280mm of the highest quality at a reasonable price is no impossibility. Just imagine what possibilities may be opened up with completely new types of lenses, based on computerized design, having several different curvatures. This could result in lens systems that we would never have imagined years ago.

Apart from the technical highlights one must not neglect other methods of improving reproduction quality, which are used as a matter of course in modern Canon lenses. For one there is the matt-black interior for more efficient

---

Available light photography – this means taking pictures in low light. This picture was taken with a 50mm, f/1.8 lens and the camera was supported on one of the pews. A zoom with a largest aperture of f/4.5 would have required six times as much exposure, which makes the use of a tripod a must. The use of flash would have totally destroyed the atmosphere.

reduction of non-image forming light or the multi-coating to improve brilliance.

You may have noticed that the front element of your EF lens appears to be multi-coloured when the light strikes it at an angle. This is due to the coating which reduces reflections that occur normally at every air/glass surface. If no coating is used, 97% of the light will be allowed through, the remainder being either lost as reflection or ghosting, causing halos and low contrast in the final image. The more elements there are in a lens system, the greater the loss due to reflections. For zoom lenses, which, by necessity, are constructed with more elements than fixed focal length lenses (Canon EF zoom lenses have up to 16 individual glasses) the sum total of light intensity lost could amount to 50% or even more. For this reason the equation 'more elements = better lens' is by no means true. The use of multi-coating can reduce reflections to a fraction of one percent. The individual coats − one for every region of the visible spectrum − are applied by vacuum deposition. The thickness of each layer is measured in a thousandth of a millimetre. Apart from reduction in reflection, the brilliance and colour saturation is preserved. A suitable choice of coatings further ensures that all EF lenses have a uniform colour rendering even if the types of glass used in individual lenses are different. Modern lens coatings are harder than the optical glasses to which they are applied but you should still be extremely careful when cleaning lens surfaces.

Finally every lens has integrated motors to drive the automatic focusing and chips to transmit the data about focal length and speed to the EOS. This is described in more detail later.

Focal Length

Two details in particular describe a lens; the focal length and the maximum aperture. Every lens is described by its

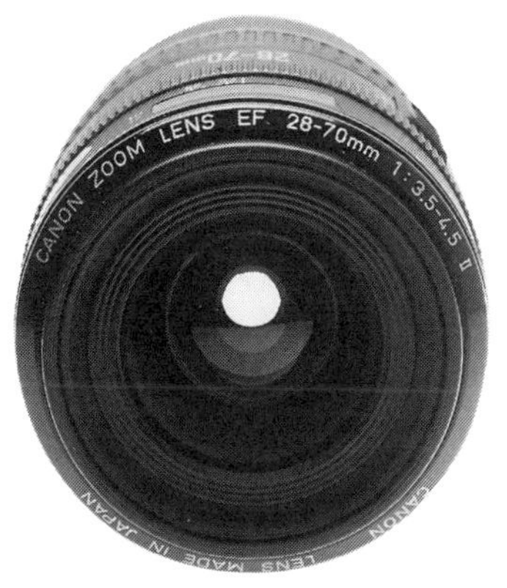

The most important lens data; focal length and maximum aperture, are engraved on the front element.

technical data, which Canon provide in the following form: EF 135mm, f/2.8 Softfocus. "EF" means that it is an autofocus lens, f/2.8 describes the largest aperture (= lens speed) and 135mm is the focal length, in this case a medium telephoto lens. Then there may be additional descriptions. In the above example it describes the option of changing the correction characteristics of this lens to obtain diffusion effects.

The possibility of being able to use the camera with different focal length lenses is the main reason for the success of SLR cameras. This opens up a wide field of creative possibilities to the photographer. Distant subjects may be brought close by using telephoto lenses. The use of a wide-angle lens captures the whole expanse of a landscape or allows shooting from close range. But these are by no means all the possibilities that different focal lengths allow. We would limit our creative possibilities if we always used a wide-angle lens for interior shots or the telephoto lens to show the clock on the church tower.

For a particular aperture, the wide-angle lens will always have a greater depth of field than the telephoto lens. By depth of field we mean the range within which a subject is sharply depicted in a photograph. As the EOS controls the aperture automatically, the effect of the wide-angle lens in this respect becomes even more noticeable.

The program curve (see chapter "Practical EOS Photo-graphy") starts to adjust the aperture as soon as the shutter speed reaches a value of 1/focal length. As the focal length of a wide-angle lens is shorter than that of a telephoto lens, the program curve will stop down the aperture much sooner than with a telephoto lens. Stopping down increases the depth of field.

This effect should be considered when using the **DEPTH** program variation. For the same depth of field a wide-angle lens has to be stopped down less than a telephoto lens, resulting in faster shutter speeds and therefore less chance of movement blur. Then there is the fact that one can use slower shutter speeds without danger of camera-shake because of the shorter focal length of wide-angle lenses.

The different effects of the various lenses can be easily identified by their focal lengths. Taken from the same shooting position, a subject will be shown twice as large when doubling the focal length of the lens, but only one quarter of the original picture area will be covered. When changing from a standard lens to a 200mm telephoto lens, only ⅛ of the picture area will be shown, but the section shown will be four times as big.

As described above, the choice of focal length influences the depth of field. One could also say that the wide-angle lens shows the main subject in close connection with its

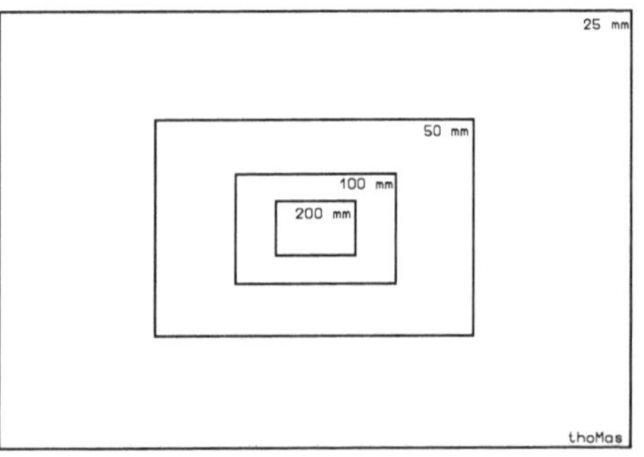

From the same shooting position a doubling of focal length means that the subject is twice as high and the area four-times the original size. The frames sketched for various focal lengths demonstrate the different representation scales for the different focal lengths. All intermediate values are possible with a zoom lens.

surroundings. With both subject and fore- and background shown sharply, the view is spatially embracing. The telephoto lens, on the other hand, lifts the subject out against an unsharp background. With increasing focal length the subject appears flatter and the spatialness is lost. Why not experiment by photographing a flower first with a wide-angle and then with a telephoto lens, then you will realize what I mean. Adjust the subject-camera distance so that with both lenses the main object is reproduced the same size.

The difference in depth of field is a phenomenon which applies universally for different focal lengths at equal reproduction scales and equal aperture. It could well be that a wide-angle shot, taken on a day with little sunlight, has a smaller depth of field than one taken under the same shooting conditions but in brighter light. If, on the other hand, you wish to keep the depth of field as small as possible it is advisable on a bright day, even with a telephoto lens, to limit it by using the **DEPTH** program variation. The same is recommended for important shots with a wide-angle lens. In rather critical conditions I would also use a tripod because a wide-angle shot generally implies that absolute sharpness in every detail is required, from close-up to infinity. Nevertheless, this should not stop you from experimenting using a wide-angle lens to obtain shallow depth of field.

Tips/Conclusion: The choice of focal length predetermines to a certain extent the depth of field. The dependence of depth of field on focal length may be described as follows:
○ The depth of field depends on the focal length; short focal lengths result in large depths of field, long focal lengths in shallow depths of field.
○ Whatever the focal length of the attached lens the depth of field is influenced by the following factors:
    a)   small aperture openings result in large depths of

field. The depth of field is doubled when doubling the f/number
   b)   long focusing distances result in large depths of field
○ Doubling the focal length means a doubling of the reproduction scale at equal shooting distance.

Perspective

The focal length of the lens and its distance from the subject determines the perspective − the way things are seen. This gave rise to the terms "wide-angle perspective" and "telephoto perspective". But these terms are quite misleading. The perspective does not change if the camera position is not changed! A telephoto lens will just show a smaller section but naturally, the impression conveyed by the picture will change and this is what is generally meant by wide-angle or telephoto perspective. However, it is incorrect.

Whatever the term used, you would be badly advised never to change your shooting position. This danger is particularly great if you possess a zoom lens. It is so easy to simply change the focal length without moving from the spot. This is often cited as a disadvantage of a zoom lens. It is unfortunate that such a wonderful facility is blamed because it is a great advantage to be able to change the reproduction scale and framing of the shot. However, you should not make the mistake of simply standing still − walk around and inspect your subject from all angles to get the best from it.

If we consider it the other way round, every focal length will probably require a different shooting position − a different perspective − to use it to its best advantage. I would recommend that you get close to your subject or further away. That, for a given subject, you determine the best shooting position for every focal length at your disposal. Now you will come to appreciate the correct

72

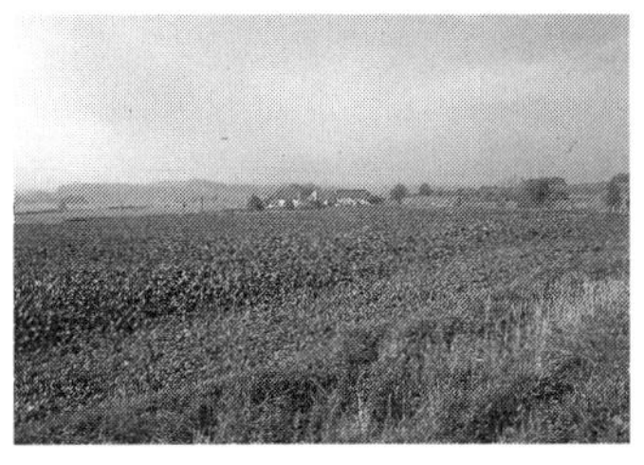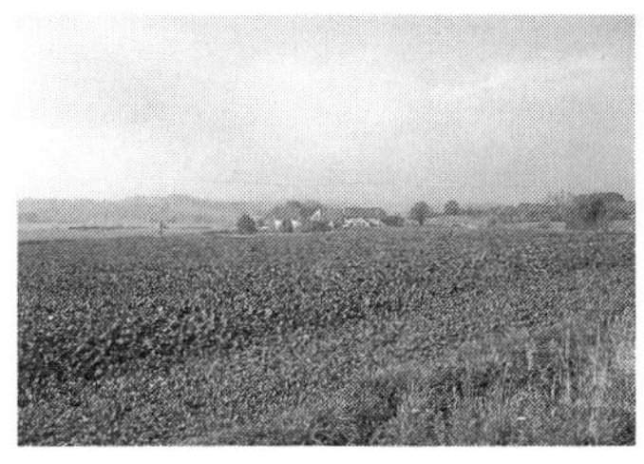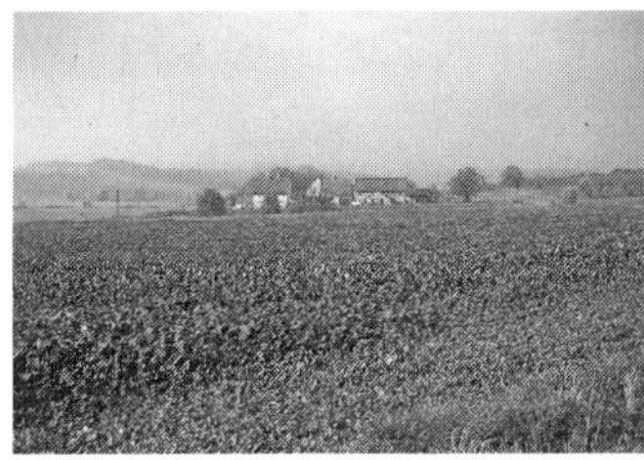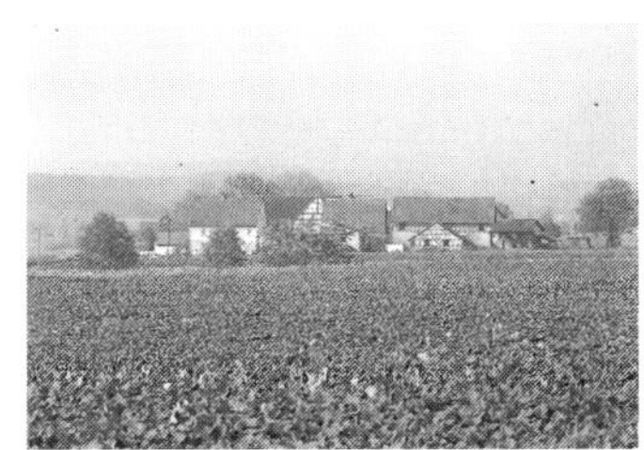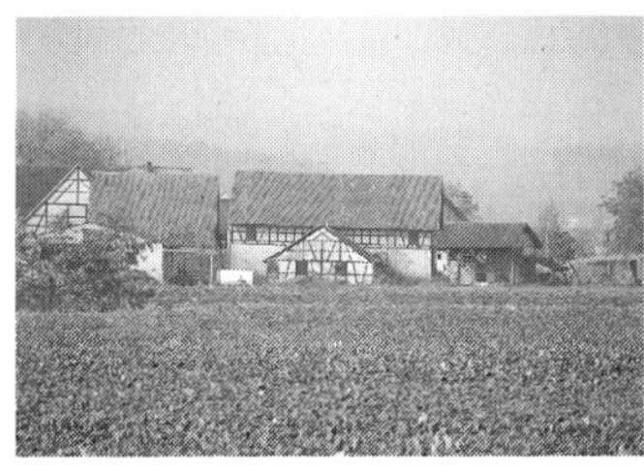

The area of subject alters with changing focal length, even if the shooting position remains the same. The perspective stays the same but the subject gets larger with the increasing focal length. If a section of a picture taken with a wide-angle lens is enlarged, it will show exactly the same perspective as the telephoto picture. The above shots were taken with the following focal lengths: 28 – 35 – 50 – 100 – and 200mm.

interpretation of the term perspective. The wide-angle perspective may be recognized by its over-emphasis on relative size. Objects at close range appear particularly large, those at a distance are relatively small.

To demonstrate this point, try a portrait, using your shortest focal length. The nose would be very close to the camera, the eyes further away, etc. The portrait would appear strange, the natural relationships distorted, the

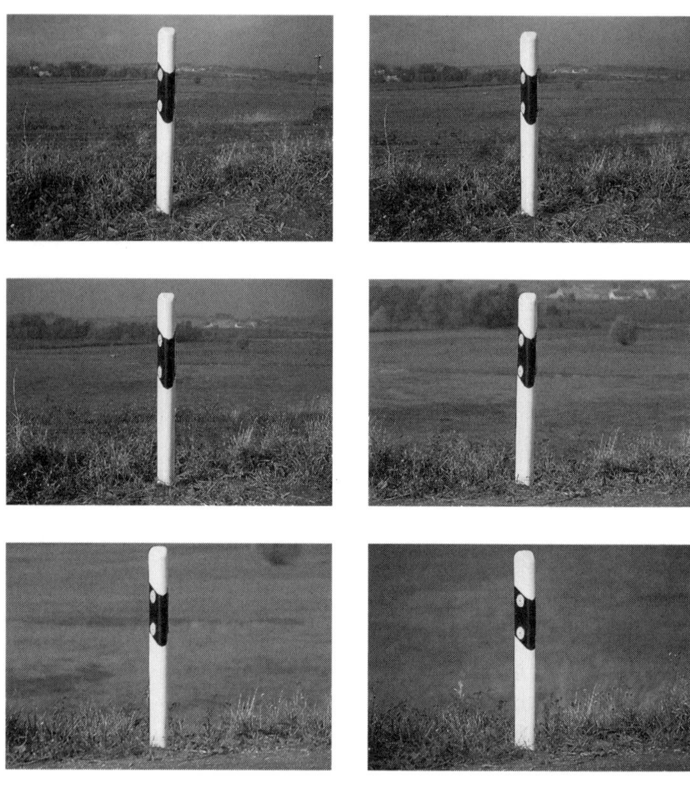

The same subject but with a considerable difference in perspective. Focal lengths used: 28 – 35 – 50 – 100 – 200 – and 300mm. The wide-angle views show the post in its surroundings, but with increasing focal length the background becomes less important and the difference in depth of field becomes very marked. The wide-angle shots are sharp from front to back. In the telephoto shots the background immediately behind the post is blurred.

whole impression rather ugly. Do go ahead and take the picture, if only for demonstration purposes. What you see through the viewfinder will appear somewhat different in the final, two-dimensional picture. Keep it for reference. Now use the same lens and photograph, say, a telephone from the side. You will notice the same distortions in the proportions, but this time the effect is quite interesting. Take this picture and keep it also for further reference.

74

This little experiment should demonstrate how one and the same effect can be both wrong in the one case and interesting in another.

The opposite happens when taking a subject with a telephoto lens from a distant viewpoint. The proportions seem to flatten − always according to subject distance. The effect is stronger, the longer the distance. Let's take a medium telephoto lens, an 85mm for example, or set the zoom ring to about 70mm. Take a portrait with this focal length at a greater distance than you would use with a 50mm lens. The proportional differences are no longer emphasised and the portrait appears particularly natural. Another benefit; the distance to the subject is now much greater for the same reproduction scale and this is particularly useful when photographing people as they don't feel crowded in and so can maintain a natural pose. If you now take a picture of the telephone it will be rather boring.

The above-described effect of the different focal lengths could be taken the other way round. It is by no means forbidden to take portraits with a wide-angle lens. Some glamour photographers favour a somewhat wide-angle lens as this makes the legs appear slim and long. And it is also quite reasonable to use a telephoto lens for subjects where it is important to avoid converging lines. There is no hard and fast general rule that will apply under any circumstances. I recommend therefore that you experiment as much as possible to explore all the possibilities.

In conclusion one could say that a wide-angle lens dramatises things, whilst a long focal length gives a more balanced view. But do take this as a very general guideline. You are the one who is taking pictures and it has to be your personality and interpretation that should shine through. What and how you see it could be contrary to what is generally taught in art classes. The choice of subject alone could be at odds with general opinion about what is a suitable subject. A landscape with threatening

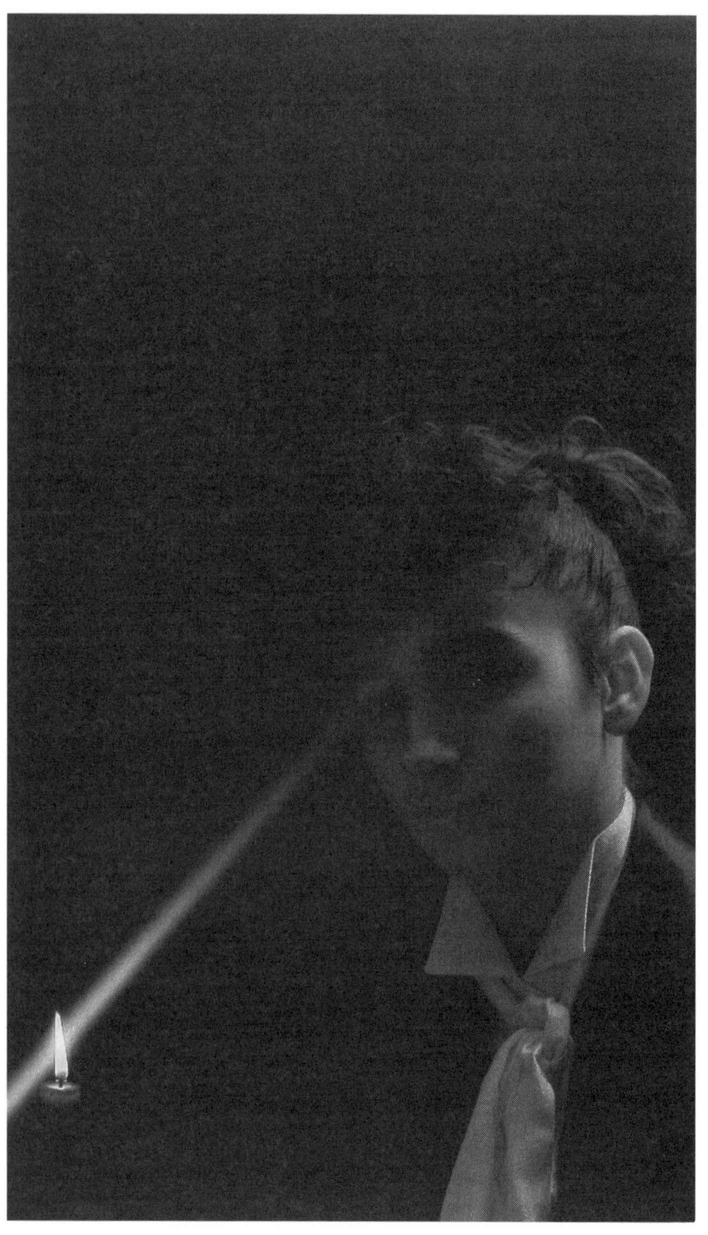

rain clouds could be even more dramatic if rendered through a wide-angle lens; the most impressive cloud formation could look rather boring through a telephoto lens. A wall with colourful graffiti might appear ordinary when taken as a general overview, but a detail picked out with the telephoto lens could have dramatic impact. Now these two examples seem to contradict what I have said at the beginning of this paragraph! The only sound conclusion is therefore; the photographer has to try to get the best out of every subject by whatever means he may think fit.

I was able to explain the special effects that characterize long and short focal lengths quite well by the above examples. But I am guilty of a serious omission — what about the standard 50mm lens? The standard lens shows everything more or less exactly as the human eye perceives it. However, it would be wrong to set standard as equal to uninteresting. Moderate would be a better term. Formerly the standard lens used to be the first choice when buying a camera. Since the introduction of the short focus zooms the 50mm fixed focal length lens has become less usual. After all, there are seven Canon zoom lenses that cover this focal length. The standard lens becomes increasingly dispensable. Now it is mainly used for applications where its particular strength — large maximum aperture — is of particular interest, or as a macro lens with a long focusing extension.

Which focal length is particularly easy to handle is a matter of opinion. You often hear the advice, 'Get close to the subject' which is generally a good idea. If it is done with a short focus lens there is the advantage of a potentially wide aperture and good depth of field but the disadvantage of severe perspective produced by the necessarily close viewpoints. The equivalents of close-up

Filters increase the impact of a picture. Entirely new aspects can be brought into being. Some expertise is required for selecting a filter; there are several dozen to choose from! If the lighting level is high, then you need a fast lens as most filters reduce the effective light level.

shots are obtainable by using a longer focal length lens and this facilitates the photography of small details but lens speed will be less and depth of field may be at a premium. However, perspective will be more gentle than results from closer viewpoints. As mentioned previously, experiment with your equipment. Don't stick rigidly to the idea that landscapes have to be taken by a wide-angle lens and portraits with a 85mm telephoto. This would mean that you disregard many an opportunity to create an interesting statement.

Lens Speed And Aperture

The lens speed describes the largest possible aperture available on a particular lens. The sequence of f/numbers, 1.4, 2, 2.8, 4 and so forth arises because aperture size is expressed as the ratio of focal length to the diameter of the aperture, stated as an f/number. This ensures that the f/number has exactly the same exposure effect with every focal length of lens. In the case of a long focal length the light has to travel a longer distance from lens to film than with a shorter focal length. This is the reason why longer focal lengths have a larger front element to allow the same amount of light to reach the film at a particular f/number.

An aperture of f/2.0 means therefore that a 50mm lens has an effective opening of 25mm (50/25 = 2.0). For a 200mm lens the effective opening would have to be 100mm (200/100 = 2.0). Now you will understand why fast telephoto lenses have such large front elements and are therefore much more expensive.

The same f/number therefore means the same amount of light being allowed to get to the film regardless of the focal length. If two lenses have different speeds, then the one with the smaller f/number is the faster one. This is a little confusing. The smaller number is the larger opening. We also talk of a small aperture meaning a small opening and conversely a large aperture means a large opening.

To avoid any confusion you should straightaway get used to referring to the aperture by its f/number.

The largest aperture of a lens is a reliable value by which the specifications of different lenses can be compared and how suitable a lens is for available-light photography. The following f/numbers describe the maximum apertures offered in the EOS range:

$$1.0 - 1.4 - 2.0 - 2.8 - 4.0 - 5.6$$

Some lenses have a maximum aperture that lies between the above values. Such intermediate values are f/1.8 and f/4.5. These are no shortcomings, but became necessary purely for optical reasons. For simpler explanation I have stated only the international aperture sequence in full stops. Reading the sequence from the left, each following value represents a halving of the lens speed. A lens with a speed of f/2.8 requires twice as much light for the same shot as a lens with an initial speed of f/2.0. In other words, the shutter speed has to be reduced to half the previous speed (danger of camera-shake) for the same subject brightness or you would have to use a film with twice the speed to use the same aperture/shutter speed combination. Simply expressed: the faster the lens speed, the later the green **P** will begin to blink and the longer you can take hand-held pictures in available light conditions.

The aperture sequence seems to be quite illogical. It would be much simpler if a doubling of the f/number (e.g. from 4 to 8) would describe a halving of the light on the film. If you remember, we have already said that this means one-quarter the light. If this is not quite clear, perhaps you could try and remember your school days and the calculation of the area of a circle. To stay with our example: a 50mm lens with aperture f/2.0, has a diameter of 25mm (50/25 = 2.0). An aperture of f/4.0 for the same lens results in a diameter of 12.5mm (50/4 = 12.5). If we now calculate the area of these two circles, then we note that the smaller circle is one-quarter the size of the bigger one. This means that the smaller opening allows only one-quarter of the light through, compared to the bigger one. If you wish, you could work out how much more light a lens with a maximum aperture of f/1.8 allows through, compared with a f/2.0 lens. Always remember, the amount of light allowed to expose the film is proportional to the area of the aperture and not the diameter.

Now you will also understand why some zoom lenses have variable maximum apertures over their range of focal lengths (e.g. f/3.5-f/4.5). The actual aperture of the zoom does not vary but the focal length does. The relative size of the opening is therefore smaller for the longer focal lengths. This difference is kept to a minimum by certain ingenious structural measures. If you take a zoom lens in your hand and look through the front element you will notice that the interior diameter of the front element increases with the increasing focal length. But, because the opening is getting larger, the lens speed remains the same or it may actually become smaller as the focal length is increased. In this way the difference in lens speed is kept to a minimum and some zoom lenses even have a constant speed throughout the entire focal length range. This is the case, for example, with the EF 100-300mm, f/5.6 Zoom.

Also note that the speed of a lens is no indication of its quality. It can't be said that the faster lens is the better one. If you remember what we have said about spherical aberration then you will understand that it is much more difficult to construct a fast lens that is of good quality than a slower one. A fast lens has, by necessity, a larger diameter and consequently the refraction differences between the central and outside light rays are particularly great. Because of the high costs of making them fast, long focus lenses of good quality are still very expensive.

I have already mentioned that the aperture of the lens is not only to define its speed, it is also used as a means of controlling the exposure and depth of field. By stopping down the aperture, less light is allowed to meet the film surface and the aperture, together with the shutter, are the means of controlling the exposure of the picture. This is automatically done for you by the EOS. As the aperture is stopped down, the depth of field is increased and this can be controlled by the **DEPTH** mode. The camera's electronics will calculate the exact amount by which the aperture has to be stopped down after the spatial depth has been determined within which the subject is to appear in sharp focus. That the ranges of the depth of field do vary may be checked in the viewfinder by attaching a wide-angle lens and then a telephoto lens and comparing the depth of field for both images.

Zoom Versus Fixed Focal Length

One can still hear statements to the effect that fixed focal length lenses are better than zoom lenses but this is not always so.

Many photographers decide, with good reason, to use a zoom lens as standard on their camera. Fixed focal lengths are increasingly used only for special applications. It is possible these days to use one zoom that covers the entire range from the wide-angle to the medium telephoto, as for example the 35-105mm offered by Canon. Not so long ago this focal length range was considered to be sufficient for every conceivable situation. This is not altogether wrong. These focal lengths are capable of covering a wide range of subjects. Formerly we had to use at least three separate lenses, 35mm, 50mm and 90mm, to cover this range but now a single lens suffices.

Our expectations have risen in line with the improvement of lens quality. We are now able to cover the range of three or four focal lengths with one zoom, but we are no longer happy with only the middle range of focal lengths. Most photographers dream about a long zoom, such as a 100-1000mm and at the other extreme a 6-45mm zoom also appears very desirable. But the photographic

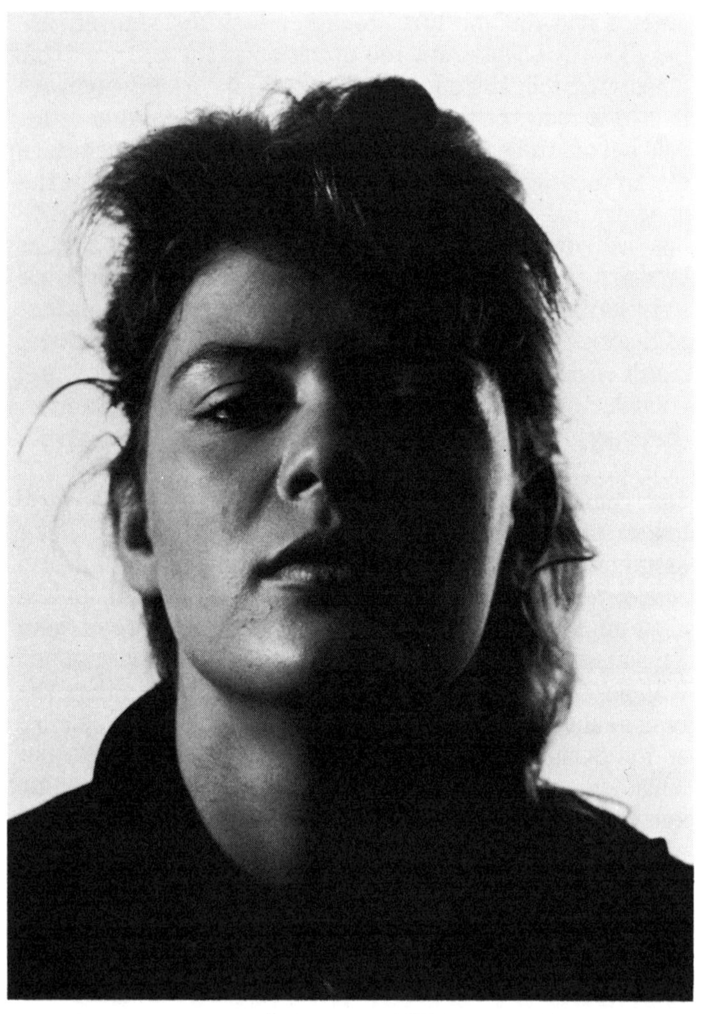

The EOS 850, the cheapest in the range of EOS cameras, does not have an integrated flash. In other respects it is equivalent to the 750.

results do not always keep pace with the increased range of focal lengths incorporated in one lens. Quite the contrary is often true. I would recommend the novice to explore initially the photographic possibilities of a moderate standard zoom, such as the 35-70mm. It is only too easy to get bogged down by technical facilities. Carrying a heavy gadget bag around and trying to decide which lens to use is more of a hindrance than a help.

If a fixed focal length lens offers the better quality, then this argument holds true even today, but only for special applications. Generally speaking the zoom lens performs just as well as the fixed focal length, sometimes even better because for comparable quality you have several focal lengths at your immediate disposal. The advantage of the fixed focal lengths lies mainly in their higher speed. Apart from that many fixed focal length lenses are constructed for special purposes, such as, for example, the macro lens or the portrait lens.

It was no coincidence that the camera depicted on the cover shows the EOS with a macro lens. Close-up and macro photography are typical areas for the fixed focal length lenses. Normal lenses are optimized for infinity. Macro lenses, on the other hand, are optimized for the close-up range and they have negligible curvature of field. This means that totally flat subjects can be photographed without loss of sharpness at the edges of pictures. For this reason these lenses are particularly suited for close-ups and copying, be this stamps, coins, maps or any other small object. There are many other fixed focal length lenses that are constructed for special applications. The most important area apart from macro photography is available-light photography, i.e. shooting without flash in situations with little light.

Lenses by Other Manufacturers

Camera manufacturers always point to possible malfunction likely to affect the camera when using lenses and accessories not of their own production. On the other hand, there is always a tempting offer of lenses which do not bear the name of Canon but are worth considering.

What are the disadvantages and advantages of using lenses by other manufacturers?

Let's start with the disadvantages. If we use accessories by other manufacturers then the camera manufacturer will refuse to furnish any guarantee that it will perform properly. This is only natural and it makes no difference whether it is flashguns or lenses.

Let's consider the worst case. An independent maker's lens on your EOS produces incorrectly-exposed pictures. All are consistently too light. It appears that the aperture control is not performing properly. The lens is sent for service and returned to you with the comment that there is no fault and the lens works properly. Then you send off the camera body with similar results. In the end you are left with a camera and a lens that do not function properly together. There is no possibility of sending them off together to check their function as a unit. However, this case is rare. Generally, accessories offered by other manufacturers perform very well; after all, they cannot afford to produce rubbish otherwise they would soon be out of business.

If you want to be absolutely sure then you should take a few test shots before committing yourself to buying one of the independent lenses. Another point to remember is that Canon lenses are standardized in respect of colour characteristics. This is not necessarily the case for lenses from other manufacturers.

The advantages, on the other hand, are often lower prices, compact construction and unusual focal lengths and speeds. Specialist manufacturers often see their chance in offering their lenses for exactly those focal lengths or applications which the camera manufacturer has not covered. My recommendation; whatever Canon offers should be bought. Only if another manufacturer offers a focal length, etc. that Canon is not offering, or the price is very tempting, would I reach for the independent lens.

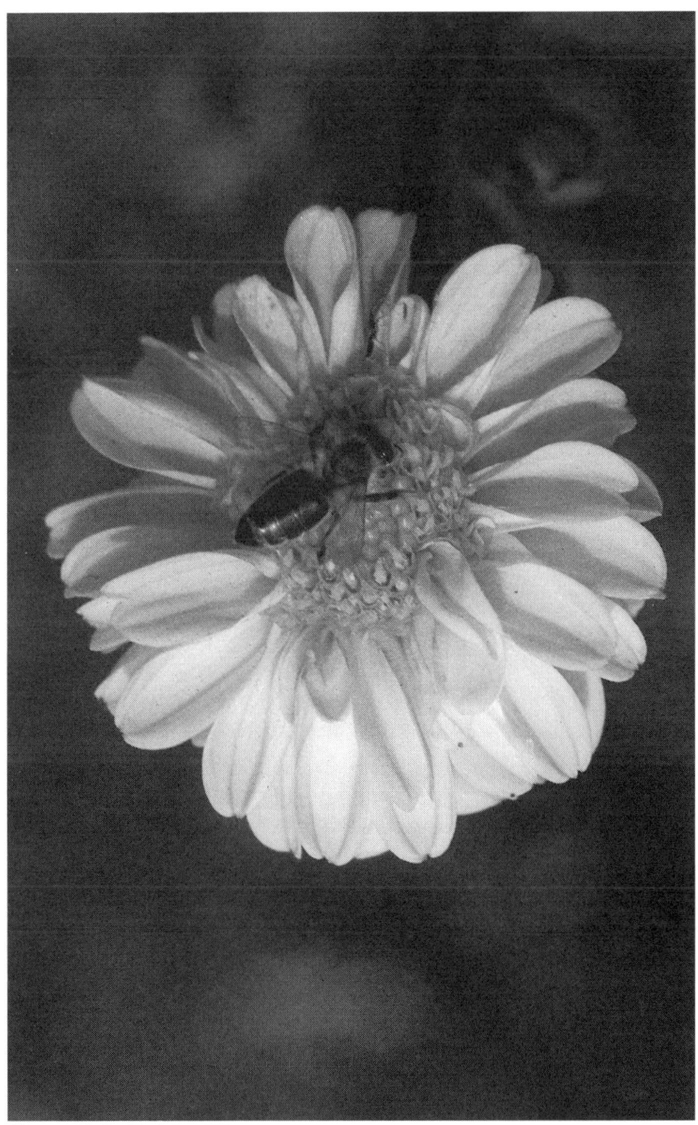

The macro setting on the EF zoom lens will be sufficient to produce close-ups at this reproduction scale. For this picture, however, the lens used was the EF 50mm, f/2.5 macro.

Lenses for the EOS

The following pages contain an overview and short description of lenses now available from Canon. One thing springs to mind; some focal length ranges seem to have been duplicated by Canon. The reasons for this are both good and not so good. If an "L" is appended to the lens description, then the good point about this lens is that it is constructed of UD glasses or fluorite. These have a particularly low dispersion and are therefore particularly brilliant in their colour rendering and picture sharpness. The bad point about it is that these types of glasses are very expensive to produce and this is reflected in the price.

Also take care whenever a lens is marked with an "A". This means it is only suitable for automatic focusing but it will be cheaper. The photographer has to do without the manual focusing facility in critical situations. When this could be important has been described in the chapter "Practical EOS photography I" under the sub heading "Autofocus". You will have to decide whether the price difference is worth the loss of manual focusing.

By the way, the use of a lens hood and UV filter is almost obligatory. The lens is protected against direct sunlight and damage. Be careful though because the front element together with the filter thread move during

---

Page 87: Architectural photographs such as this call for a rather long focus lens to avoid distortion. This shot was taken at an angle from below and converging lines were avoided thanks to the 300mm lens and distant viewpoint.

Page 88: It is worth while moving around the subject, investigating it from all angles. Both shots were taken within a short time of each other as I only turned round! Even the normal program mode will produce great depth of field if a wide-angle lens is attached, as the shutter speed/ aperture combination is selected in accordance with the focal length.

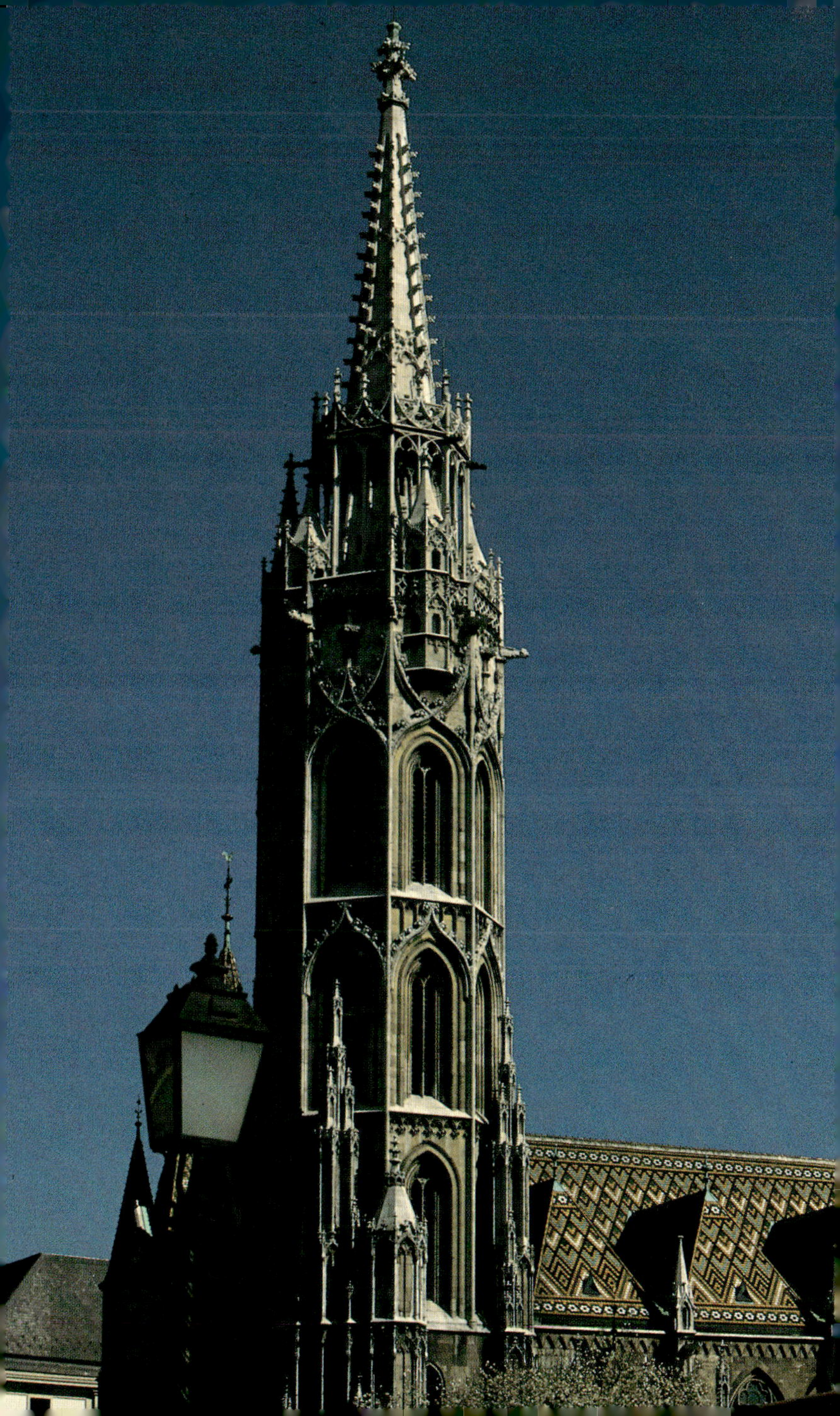

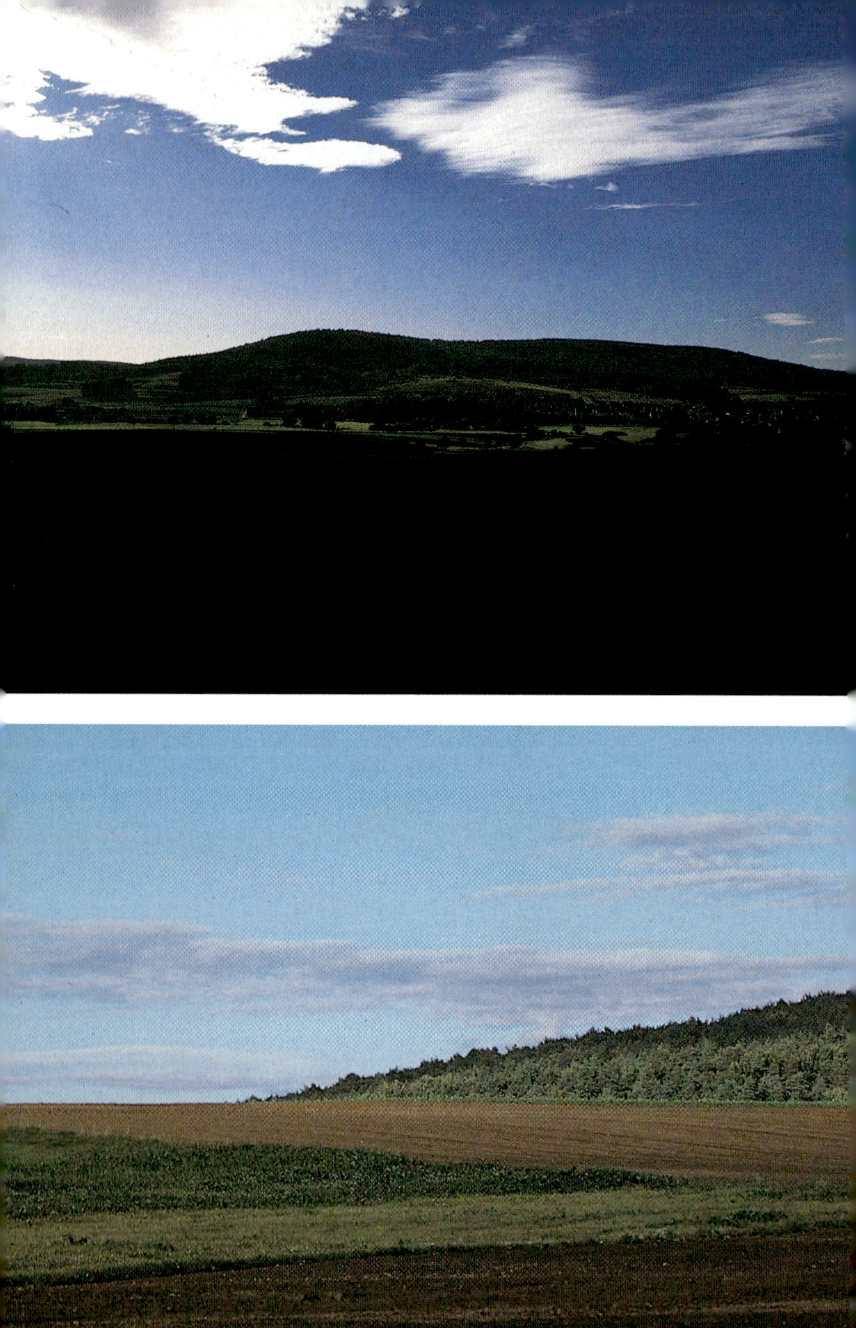

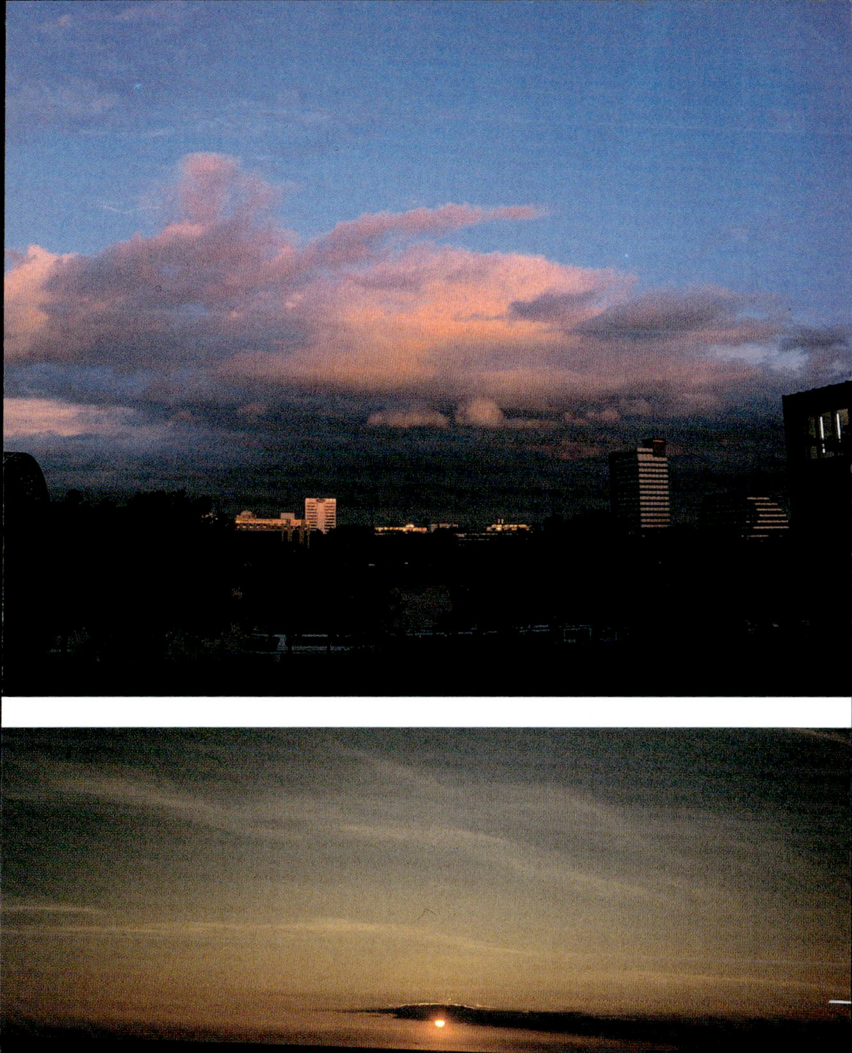

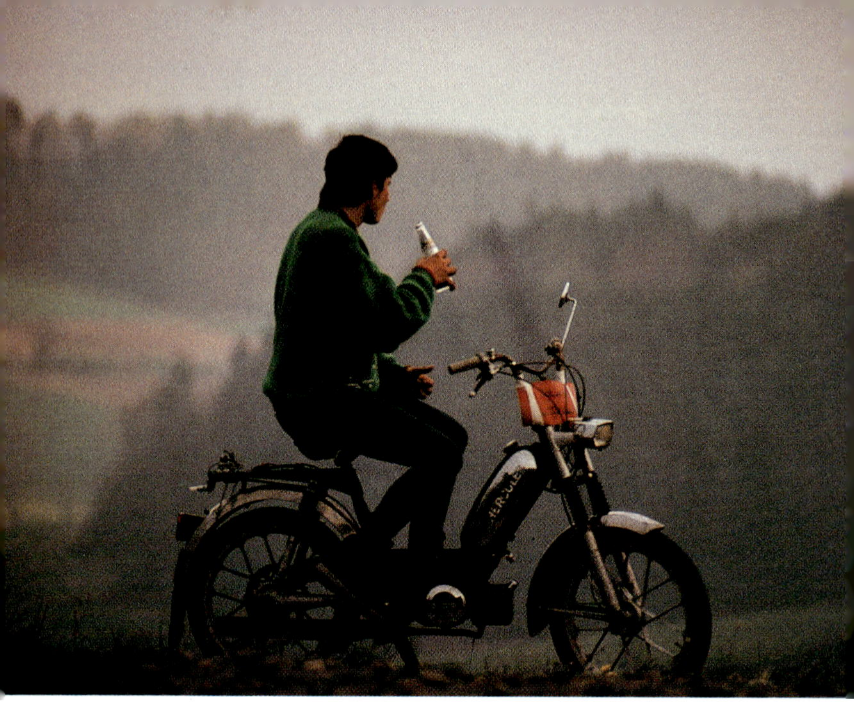

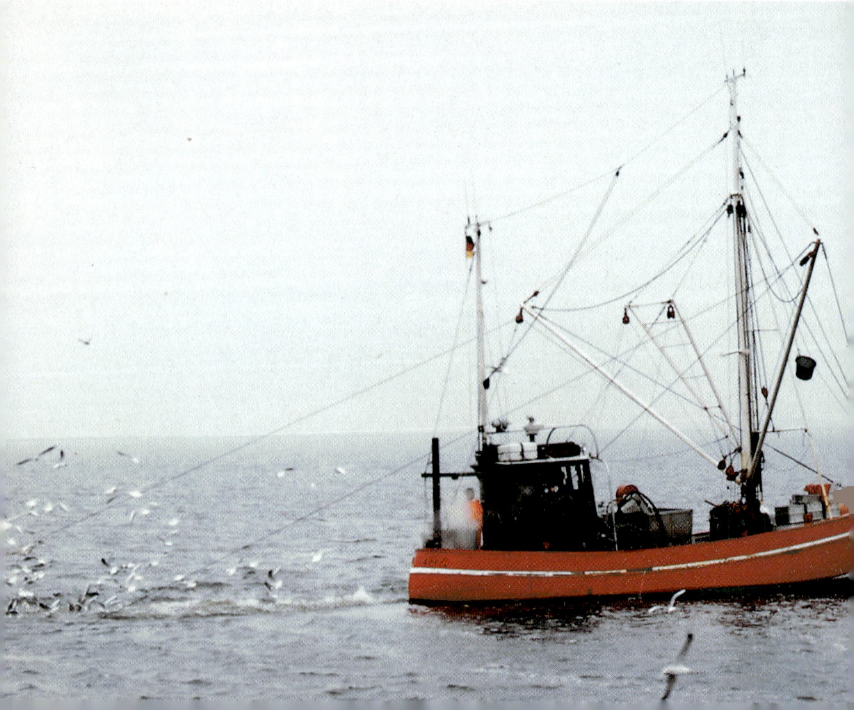

focusing on some EF zoom lenses and an attached hood could block the movement of the zoom ring. It could also negate the effects of certain filters.

Wide-Angle Lenses – The New Look

Canon's fixed focal length lenses are excellent. It is a sheer delight to behold these optical marvels – unfortunately the joy is marred when one looks at the price! Only the standard lens is not well represented, a faster alternative to the 50mm, f/1.8 would be most welcome.

At present Canon are offering three lenses in the wide-angle range which are all excellent because of their fast speed of f/2.8. The Fisheye EF 15mm, f/2.8 is an extreme wide-angle lens which covers the entire picture frame despite its extreme angle of view of 180°. If you stretch your arms sideways you will embrace the angle that this lens covers. Such a lens is not easy to use because you have to be careful that no parts of your body intrude into the picture. If the sun is behind you your shadow will certainly be in the picture. Because of the large angle of view one has to be particularly careful to exclude unwanted items.

Due to optical principles, straight lines tend to be curved by a wide-angle lens. This phenomenon is more pronounced, the shorter the focal length. Only those lines that run through the centre of the frame are not bent. This

---

Page 89: *Sunsets are very popular subjects and with every justification. The truth of this is demonstrated by these two views. The amateur will be very encouraged if he manages to recognize and shoot pictures like these.*

Page 90: *Two pictures to prove that all weather conditions can be suitable for photography.*

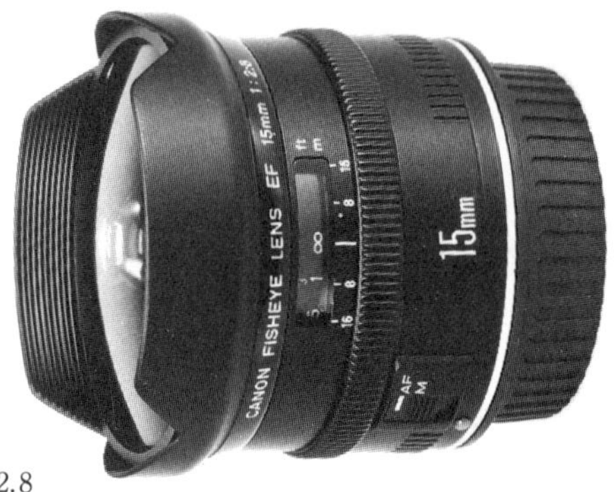

Canon Fisheye EF 15mm, f/2.8

is not a reproduction error of the lens, but an inevitable consequence of optical laws. In the fisheye lens, which has the shortest focal length in the EF program, this barrel distortion is particularly noticeable. This type of lens must be used sparingly because of its peculiar imagery, which could become quite objectionable after a while. Fisheye lenses are suitable for panoramic views, in very restricted spaces and for special effects.

Used carefully and with a particular special effect in mind, the fisheye lens can produce the most unusual and striking images but you will have to be careful not to overdo this special effect. For this reason I would recommend the purchase of this lens only to the very dedicated photographer who has the complete range of focal lengths at his disposal and who needs this lens for a particular project.

Then there is the EF 24mm, f/2.8 wide-angle lens with an angle of view of 84°. This lens gives considerable depth of field even at fully open aperture and it is capable of most impressive wide-angle images. The curvature of lines at the edge of the picture is still noticeable but is not nearly so severe as with the fisheye lens.

The EF 28mm, f/2.8 wide-angle produces almost no distortion. It is very fast, possesses aspherical elements and you can expect excellent reproduction quality. If your

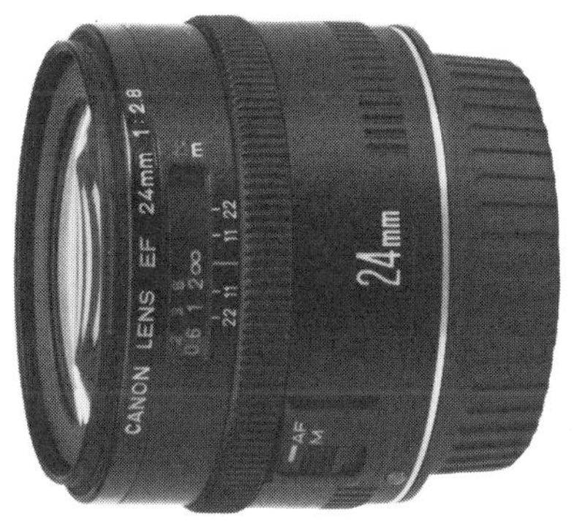

Canon Wide-angle EF 24mm, f/2.8

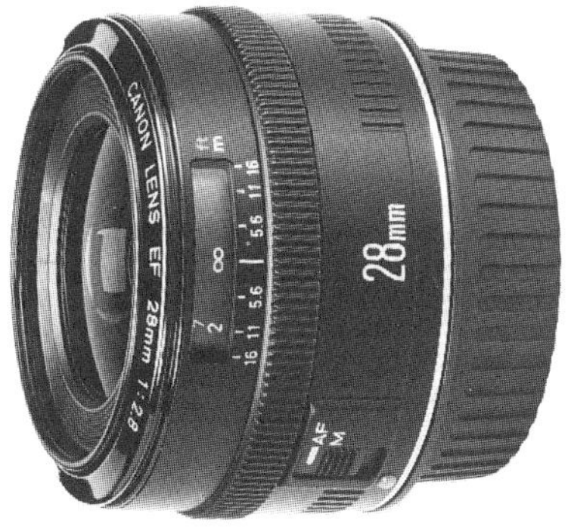

Canon Wide-angle EF 28mm, f/2.8

standard zoom does not have this focal length then I recommend that this lens is your first purchase in the wide-angle range. Unlike the 35mm lens, whose characteristics are still quite normal, this focal length clearly possesses the wide-angle characteristics without being extreme in its effect.

Standard but not Boring

The greatest advantage of the EF 50mm, f/1.8 is its price. Compared to the zoom lenses it is very fast but for a standard lens it could be considered not fast enough. Normally we would expect speeds of f/1.2 or f/1.4 for

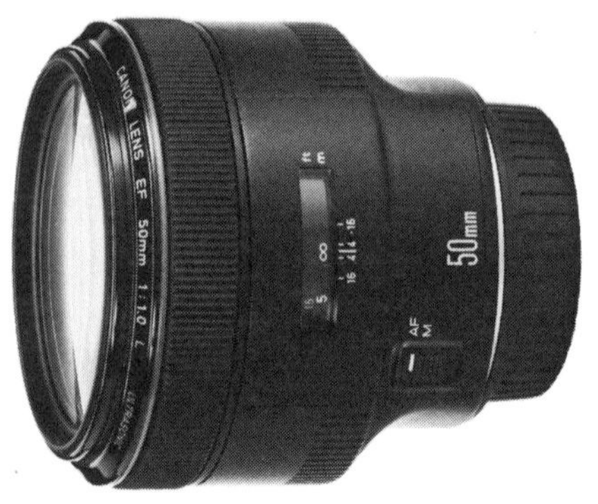

Canon EF 50mm, f/1.8

standard lenses, as Canon offer for their non AF range of cameras. The f/1.8 is generally offered as a reasonably-priced alternative. I do not understand why Canon have not also followed this principle for their EF lenses but I hope they will soon provide a faster alternative. Their production policy is rather difficult to understand, particularly as they have announced their intention of developing the EF 50mm, f/1.0 lens as the crowning glory in their production range. When this will be on the market is still uncertain.

The only possibility of advancing into the close-up range with a EOS camera at present is with the Compact Macro EF 50mm, f/2.5. Its extra long extension allows reproduction ratios of up to 1:2 (half life size) without the need of any accessories.

The long extension is not the only reason that makes this lens particularly useful for the close range. The whole optical construction is of the highest quality. A macro lens has to be suitable for copying and this makes special demands on the quality of a lens; it has to be free from distortions, no curvature of field, and it has to produce true colours and have highest possible resolution. These constraints ensure the very best quality of lens for the close range but which is also suitable for general photography.

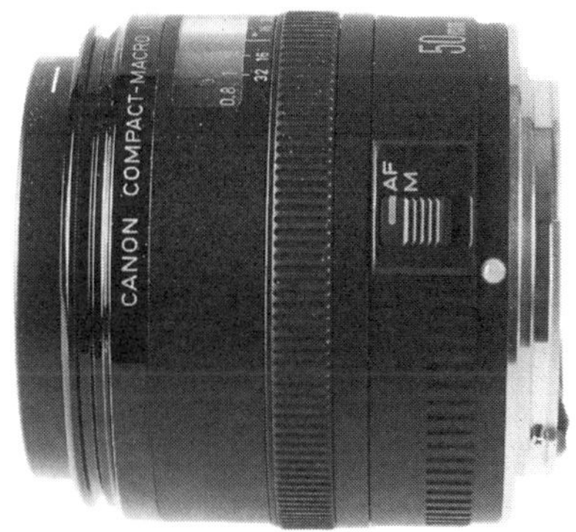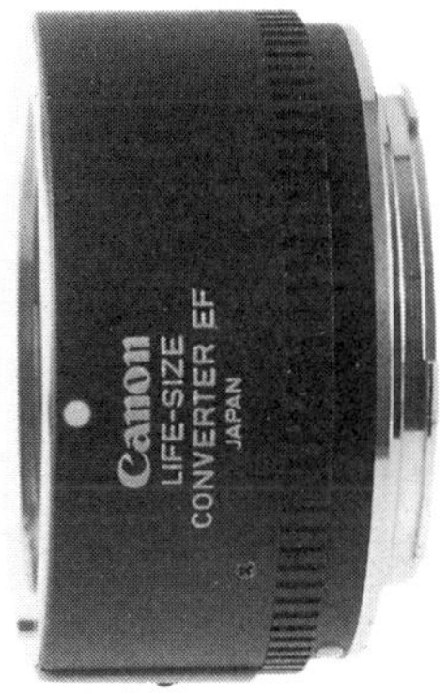

Canon EF 50mm, f/2.8 Macro and Life-Size Converter

The Life-Size Converter EF, suitable as an accessory for the macro lens, is used, as the name indicates, to bring the reproduction scale down to 1:1, i.e. down to actual size.

The Romantic View by Soft Focus Lens

The 135mm, f/2.8 lens is a very interesting addition to the range of lenses. In this case the carefully calculated optical quality of the lens can be intentionally impaired — for a good reason though! If you possess such a lens you can convince yourself of the fatal effects of spherical aberration. The soft focus lens makes use of this optical error to introduce a soft focus effect of varying degree.

This effect is often used in portrait photography as it helps to cover up small blemishes such as unclear skin and wrinkles. Not only portraits benefit from a soft rendering. A landscape, a woodland scene in autumn, a nude or a still-life are all examples which could benefit from the rendering of the soft focus lens.

It would be wrong to consider the soft focus lens imperfectly corrected. On the contrary, at its basic setting it is quite a normal, excellently-corrected lens which can

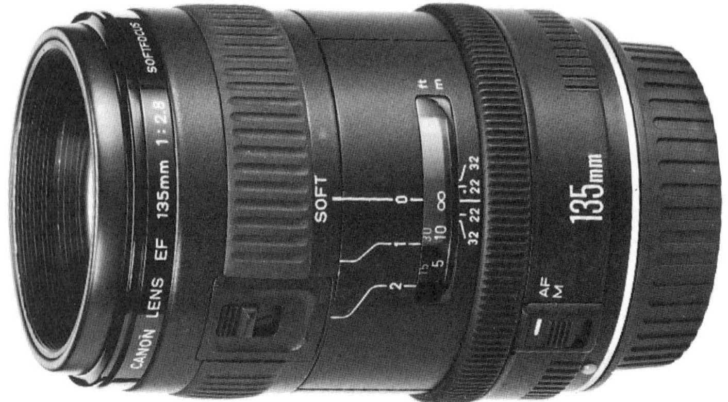

Canon EF 135mm, f/2.8 Soft focus

be used just as any other high-quality telephoto lens.

As there are other, much cheaper, means of obtaining soft focus effects — from a nylon stocking to vaseline on filter — you should ask yourself whether you really need this specialist lens. All of these devices depend very much on the aperture and the effect is greatest when it is fully open.

Tip: For your initial attempts at soft focus I would recommend you simply to breath gently on the front element just before making the exposure. The effect can be varied by how much condensation is on the front element when the shot is taken.

When using this lens the degree of the soft focus effect can be modified by stopping down. However, there is virtually no effect at all at f/5.6 and smaller apertures. When using this lens with a 750 or 850 you will have to take care that the lighting is not too bright, otherwise the program mode will determine apertures that are too small. In this case it would be better if the aperture could be preset to be able to determine exactly the soft focus effect.

Super-Fast Giants

Canon's long telephoto lenses are real photographic gems. Exceedingly fast for the focal length, they are all constructed with aspherical elements and include special glasses. The EF 200mm, f/1.8 has the same speed as the standard lens and is, as such, particularly suited to available light and the photography of interiors. You will find suitable subjects at the zoo, the theatre or opera, and at the fun fair. Because of its high speed, this lens, together with one of the two extenders, is useful in many situations. The EF 300mm, f/2.8 is the lens for sports and wild-life photographers. The high speed makes faster shutter speeds possible to capture rapid movements. The EF 600mm, f/4.0 is the longest focus telephoto lens available. If you have a steady hand and good light, you may just about be able to take hand-held shots with this lens, the only handicap being a weight of six kilos!

All three lenses use aspherical elements and UD glasses or fluorite, resulting in very low dispersion. I have already described the advantages of aspherical elements. Apart from spherical, there is also chromatic, aberration. This means that the different spectral colours are differently refracted through glass. This, in turn, leads to colour fringes as the focal point for blue light is slightly in front of, and that of red light is slightly behind, the focusing plane. In special glasses, such as UD or fluorite, this difference is negligible and the differences in the focal plane of these colours is not noticeable. Lenses using such glasses produce sharper pictures with higher colour saturation.

Chromatic aberration can also be corrected by suitably-shaped lenses and special types of glass. Furthermore, this problem is reduced by keeping the speed to a reasonable value so you need not worry unduly that a lens constructed without this type of glass would be unsuitable. However, a long focus telephoto lens with high speed,

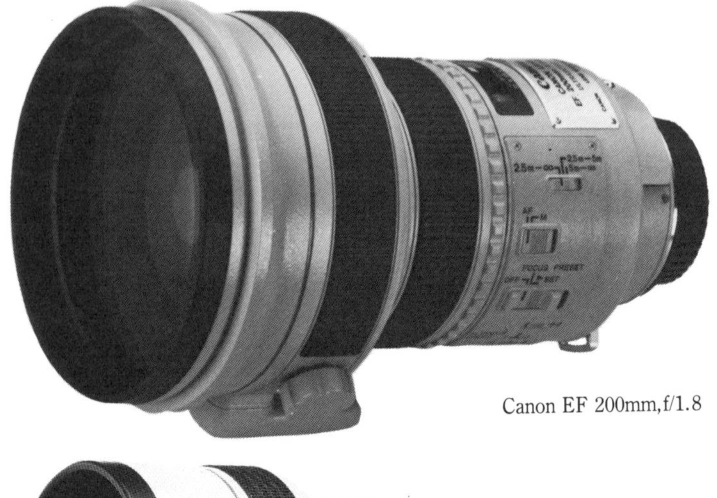

Canon EF 200mm, f/1.8

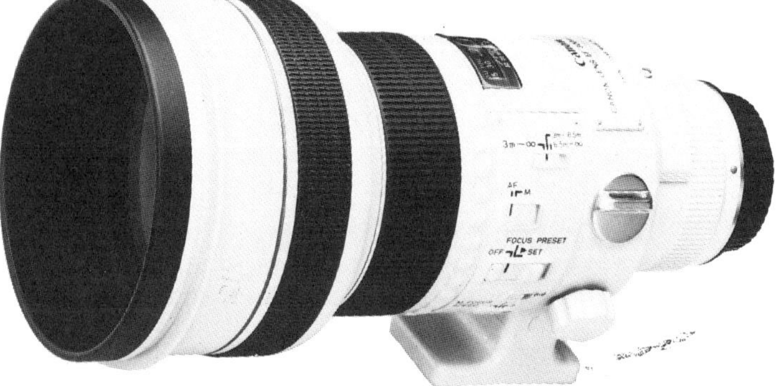

Canon EF 300mm, f/2.8 L

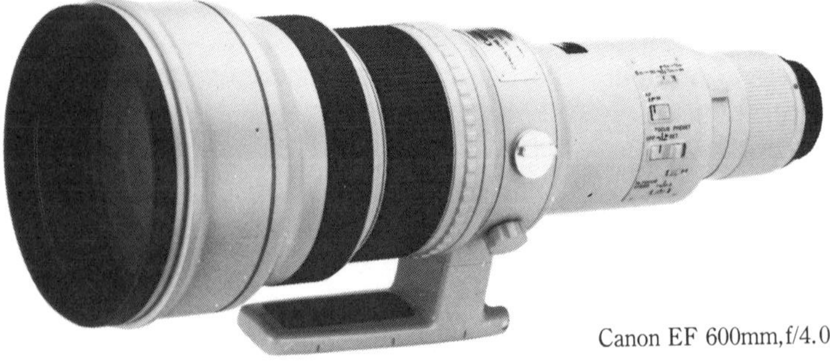

Canon EF 600mm, f/4.0

using aspherical elements and special types of glass, will produce the best results.

To appreciate the high speed of these EF lenses you should realise that the 200mm lens is as fast as the standard lens but with four times the focal length! All three telephoto lenses represent the very best in lens construction.

Two extenders are available for these three long lenses. They extend the focal length of the lens used by a factor of 1.4 or 2 respectively. This increases the lens range offered by Canon quite considerably. An EF 1200mm, f/8.0 (EF 600mm, f/4.0 with the Extender EF 2X) is quite a powerful tool!

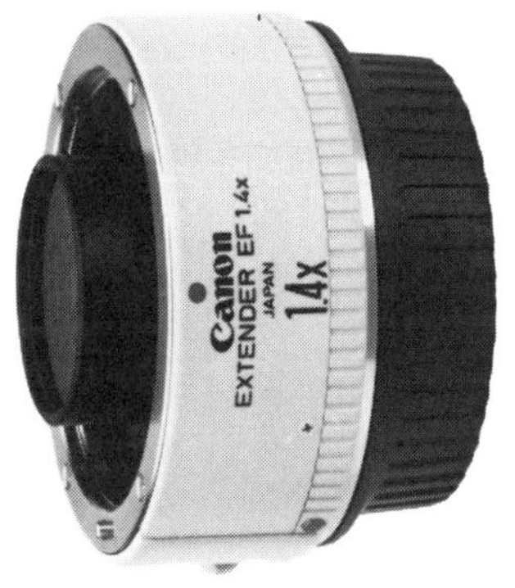

Canon Extender EF 1.4X

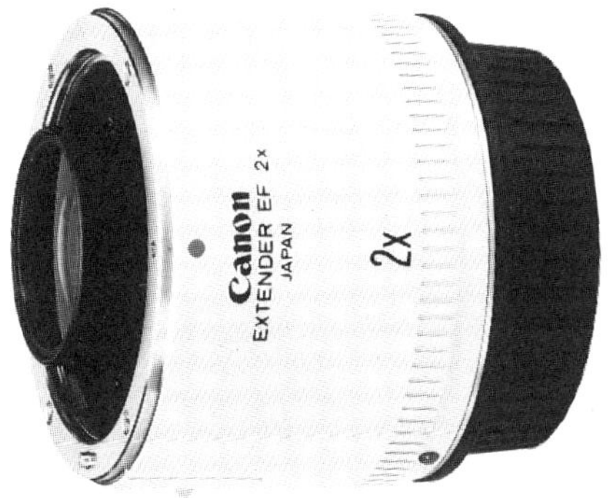

Canon Extender EF 2X

This example of 1200mm, f/8.0 quite clearly demonstrates the disadvantages of an extender. By extending the focal length the speed is reduced by the same factor. The use of the extender reduces the amount of light that can expose the film. You can calculate this for yourself. I have already given you the formula.

The question of reduced speed is not a big problem with the above three telephoto lenses. They are so fast that even with an extender the resulting shutter speeds should be suitable for a wide range of situations. A 280mm, f/2.5 (200mm, f/1.8 plus Extender EF 1.4X) or a 400mm, f/3.6 (200mm, f/1.8 plus Extender EF 2X) are still extremely fast lenses. The same holds true for the other focal lengths. The extenders may therefore be used with these lenses to turn their focal lengths into three different lenses. Any loss in quality, which the use of an extender by necessity involves, is almost negligible as Canon have specially developed these two extenders for the three telephoto lenses. This ensures that converter and lens perform together as a perfect optical unit. Theoretical loss in quality is not relevant as I can say with some certainty that you would find it difficult to discern any difference in pictures taken with or without a converter. The following combinations are possible:

Lens	+ EF Extender 1.4X	+ EF Extender 2X
200mm, f/1.8 L	280mm, f/2.5	400mm, f/3.6
300mm, f/2.8 L	420mm, f/3.9	600mm, f/5.6
600mm, f/4.0 L	840mm, f/5.6	1200mm, f/8.0

Always Variable: Zoom Lenses

There is plenty of choice of variable focal length lenses by Canon. The range between 28mm to 300mm is covered completely.

The wide-angle and standard focal length range is covered by the EF 28-70mm, f/3.5-4.5 zoom. If you are not particularly interested in the more extreme wide-angle views you will be well served by this lens. It could be complemented by a zoom in the telephoto range to provide total coverage.

The EF 35-70mm, f/3.5-4.5 is the typical standard zoom, which can be used universally, provided its slow speed is no hindrance. This lens is particularly handy as it is hardly heavier than a standard fixed focal length lens and is nearly as compact. It covers the medium focal length range. The 35mm end allows reasonably large angles of view without the typical wide-angle effects. At the other extreme it is capable of showing subject detail at medium distances. This zoom is easy to use so is ideal as a universal lens for the novice. Canon offer two versions of this focal length, one with and one without a facility for

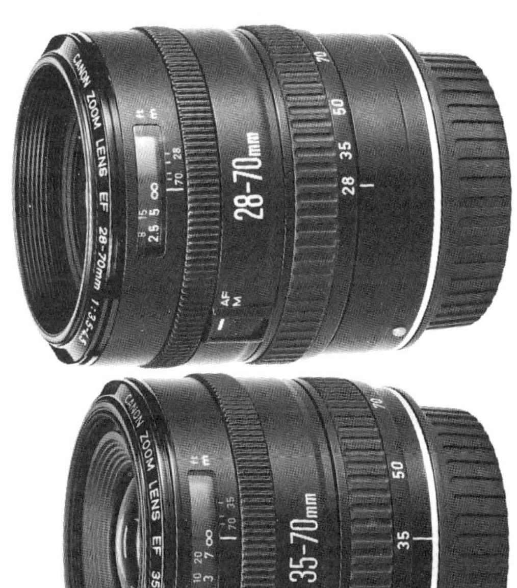

Canon Wide-angle
Zoom EF
28-70mm, f/3.5-4.5

Canon Wide-angle
Zoom EF
35-70mm, f/3.5-4.5

manual focusing (EF 35-70mm, f/3.5-4.5 A is autofocus only).

The two zoom lenses that cover the wide-angle range up to the real telephoto range are the EF 35-105mm, f/3.5-4.5 and the EF 35-135mm, f/3.5-4.5. Either of these two zooms should satisfy most of your requirements as they both cover an important range of focal lengths. For general photography no other focal length is needed. If you have a particular field of interest, then perhaps one more fixed focal length lens in the wide-angle or telephoto range would constitute the ideal complement to either of these zoom lenses.

The EF 70-210mm, f/4.0 is a most popular zoom lens. The introduction of this range of focal lengths contributed to the great success of zoom lenses. Together with, say,

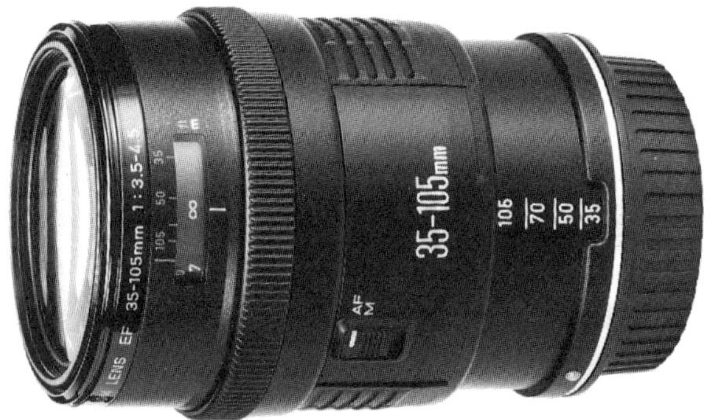

Canon Wide-angle Zoom EF 35-105mm, f/3.5-4.5 zoom

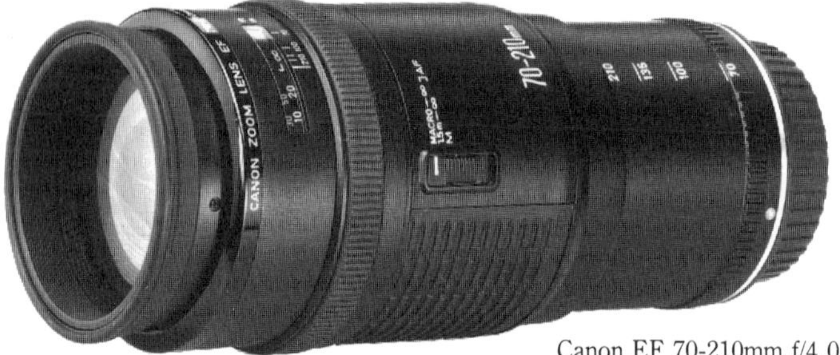

Canon EF 70-210mm, f/4.0

the EF 28-70mm, f/3.5-4.5 standard zoom you can cover the entire range from wide-angle to telephoto. All the focal lengths that are of interest are covered; the 85-105mm range for portraits, and the 200mm focal length for real telephoto effects with shallow depth of field and emphasis of the main subject against a blurred background.

If you choose the EF 50-200mm, f/3.5-4.5 instead, then the standard lens is superfluous unless the higher speed is of particular importance. This lens covers an angle of view of 12° to 46° and therefore the entire range from the standard to the telephoto focal lengths. Longer focal lengths are needed only for special applications such as sports and animal photography.

The same focal length is provided in an "L" version marked with a red ring. The construction of this variation includes elements with extremely low dispersion, the advantages of which have already been described. The extra cost of the EF 100-300mm, f/5.6 L can only be justified if you need extreme enlargements. It is directed at the professional market where slides are projected on large screens and exhibited to the public. The normal lens is of excellent quality and to buy the "L" version purely to enlarge the negatives to a 9 x 13cm format is ridiculous.

Two other long zooms, the EF 100-200mm, f/4.5 and the EF 100-300mm, f/5.6 are of excellent construction. The latter is also available in an "L" version. Either of these lenses would complement a standard zoom, for example the 35-70mm, or a standard fixed focal length.

When considering the EF 100-200mm, f/4.5 A, you will have to take into account that this lens cannot be focused manually.

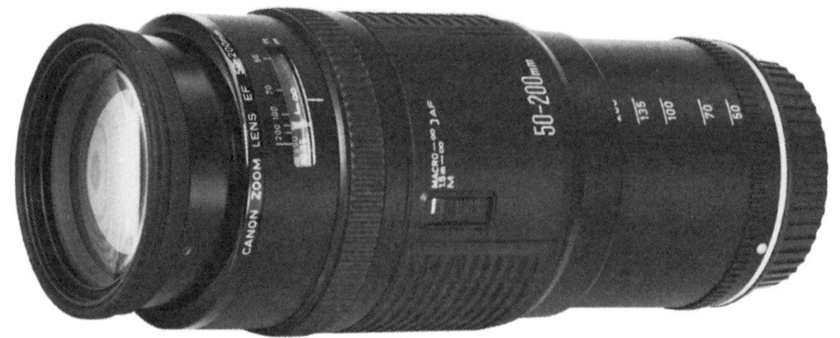

EF 50-200mm, f/3.5-4.5

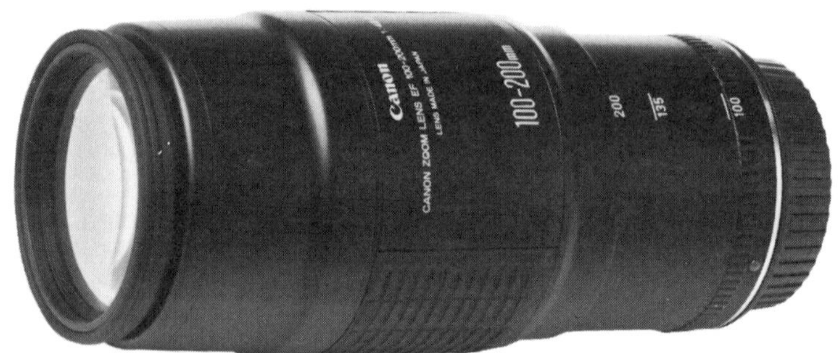

EF 100-200mm, f/4.5 A

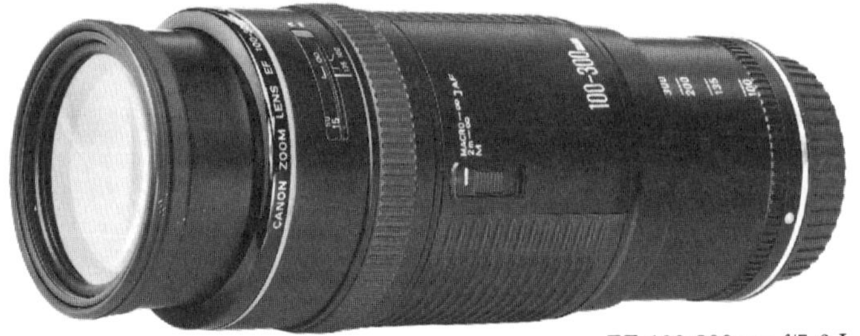

EF 100-300mm, f/5.6 L

The Canon EOS Lenses

Objektivtyp	Autofokus-Motor		Bild-winkel	Linsen/ Glieder	Kleinste Blende	Kürzeste Aufnahme-distanz (m)	Filter-Ø (mm)	Länge (mm)	Gewicht (g)
	AFD	USM							
EF 2.8/15 mm Fish-Eye	●		180°	8/7	22	0.2	Filterhalter	62.2	330
EF 2.8/24 mm	●		84°	10/10	22	0.25	58	48.5	270
EF 2.8/28 mm	●		75°	5/5	22	0.3	52	42.5	185
EF 1.8/50 mm	●		46°	6/5	22	0.45	52	42.5	190
EF 2.5/50 mm Makro	●		46°	9/8	32	0.23	52	63.0	280
EF 2.8/135 mm Softfokus	●		18°	7/6	32	1.3	52	98.4	390
EF 1.8/200 mm L		●	12°	12/10	22	2.5	48	208.0	3000
EF 2.8/300 mm L		●	8°15'	9/7	32	3	48	253.0	2850
EF 4.0/600 mm L		●	4°10'	9/8	32	6	48	456.0	6000
EF 3.5-4.5/28-70 mm	●		75°-34°	10/9	22-29	0.5	52	75.6	285
EF 3.5-4.5/35-70 mm	●		63°-34°	9/8	22-29	0.5	52	63.0	245
EF 3.5-4.5/35-70 mm A	●		63°-34°	9/8	22-29	0.39	52	63.0	230
EF 3.5-4.5/35-105 mm	●		63°-23°30'	14/11	22-29	1.2	58	81.9	400
EF 3.5-4.5/35-135 mm	●		63°-18°	16/12	22-29	1.5	58	94.5	475
EF 3.5-4.5/50-200 mm	●		46°-12°	16/13	22-29	1.5	58	146.4	690
EF 3.5-4.5/50-200 mm L	●		46°-12°	16/14	22-29	1.5	58	145.8	695
EF 4.0/70-210 mm	●		34°-11°45'	11/8	32	1.5	58	137.6	605
EF 4.5/100-200 mm A	●		24°-12°	10/7	32-29	1.9	58	130.5	520
EF 5.6/100-300 mm	●		24°-8°15'	15/9	32	2	58	166.8	685
EF 5.6/100-300 mm L	●		24°-8°15'	15/10	32	2	58	166.6	695
Extender EF 1,4 X	–	–	–	5/4	–	–	–	27.3	200
Extender EF 2 X	–	–	–	7/5	–	–	–	50.5	240
Life-Size Konverter EF	–	–	–	4/3	–	–	–	34.9	160

1. Die Extender EF 1.4 X und EF 2 X sind exklusiv für den Einsatz mit den EF-Objektiven EF 1,8/200 mm L, EF 2,8/300 mm L und EF 4,0/600 mm L vorgesehen.
2. Der Life-Size-Konverter EF ist exklusiv für das Makroobjektiv 2,5/50 mm vorgesehen und erlaubt Aufnahmemaßstäbe bis 1:1.
3. Alle EF-Zoomobjektive haben eine Makro-Einstellung eingebaut.
4. AFD = Bogenmotor (Arc Form Drive). USM = Ultraschallmotor (Ultra Sonic Motor).
5. ● Bedeutet: in kurzer Zeit lieferbar.

Practical EOS Photography II — More Theory

'What's the use of this?' you may ask. 'I simply press the button and the camera does the rest. Why do I have to bother with photographic theory?'. Don't worry, I do not intend to give you a lecture on theory. My intentions are to help you to get to know more about your EOS in particular and photography in general. This glimpse behind the scenes should help you appreciate the internal technical processes and therefore improve your photographic technique. I find it quite fascinating to know what happens when I press the release, particularly as the EOS 750/850 cameras do not inform you of any settings apart from the green **P** and dot in the viewfinder. If you know what function the aperture performs in the lens, what effect the shutter speed has, how to control depth of field, then it is easier to understand the internal functions of the EOS and to improve your technique.

The slogan of just simply pushing the button was coined at the beginning of this century when it heralded the beginnings of photography as a popular hobby. Kodak advertised their camera, that already had a film loaded in the factory, with the slogan; 'You press the button — we do the rest'. You made 100 exposures then sent the camera, still with the film inside, back to Kodak who developed and printed the negatives and returned them and the prints to you, together with the camera loaded with a fresh film. This camera was very reasonably priced, compared with others, and easy to handle. The complete novice was presented for the first time with the opportunity to take pictures without having to know much about photography. Photography had stepped out from the élite circle of experts to meet the whole world.

It may sound strange when I say that a "simple" camera

like the EOS presents us with more challenges than the early Kodak box camera. For a start, we have to select the right film and decide on a suitable lens. But don't worry. Simple handling was the brief that the EOS designers had to meet. The photographic facilities, on the other hand, have marched forward in step with technological developments.

This is how it ought to be. It would be altogether wrong to make a problem out of every exposure. The fascination of modern photography lies to some extent in the fact that we can concentrate fully on the subject without having to bother too much about the theory. On the other hand, there will always be situations where even the most sophisticated camera will produce failures which could have been avoided if we had considered everything properly before taking the shot. After all, the camera has been programmed according to certain principles. It cannot think for itself. In the majority of cases its decisions will be reasonably correct, but not always perfect. Sometimes they will be wrong, and, life being what it is, this will probably be when perfection is really important.

If, for example, a certain statement has to be made, then the photographer will have to decide beforehand what the final photograph should look like. This is only possible if you know what the EOS will do, how and when. We can then take its characteristics into consideration and use them for our specifically defined needs.

The Single Lens Reflex Camera

The EOS is an SLR (single lens reflex) camera with TTL exposure metering and program mode with open aperture metering. SLR means that the image projected by the lens is reflected by a mirror onto the focusing screen. The image on the screen is reversed left to right and is inverted by the prism to appear in the viewfinder the right way round. If you don't believe that this is so, check what happens in a slide projector. Here too, the slide has to be inserted upside down to be projected the right way up on the screen. To check that everything is indeed reversed in a mirror, hold up a newspaper to it. To read it you would have to master the art of reading from right to left.

An important element of the camera is situated between the mirror and the prism and is the focusing screen that makes the image visible to us. The distance between the lens and focusing screen must be the same as the distance from lens to film plane. Only then can you be certain that a sharp image on the focusing screen also corresponds to a sharp photograph. The focusing screen of the EOS is of a very special type. It has been produced by a laser process and this method is the reason for the particularly brilliant viewfinder image.

The advantage of this engineering effort becomes immediately clear when looking through the viewfinder. The image seen is clear and bright and corresponds exactly to what will be represented on film, with one restriction; the extent of the viewfinder image is only 92% of the final negative. This measure was taken to ensure that the final photograph will show every detail right to the edge, just as the photographer saw it in the viewfinder.

As soon as the release is activated, the mirror folds away and the shutter is opened, allowing the light free passage to expose the film. The aperture is stopped down at the same time to the required value.

It is the shutter's duty to limit the time that the light is allowed to expose the film and the iris diaphram's duty is to restrict the amount of light by closing the aperture to a certain size. The combination of aperture (intensity of light) and shutter speed (duration of light) controls the exposure (the amount of light) that will meet the film emulsion and so produce the image. The task of controlling the exposure is performed by the program mode, which selects a suitable aperture and shutter speed, calculated for the appropriate film speed and subject brightness. The

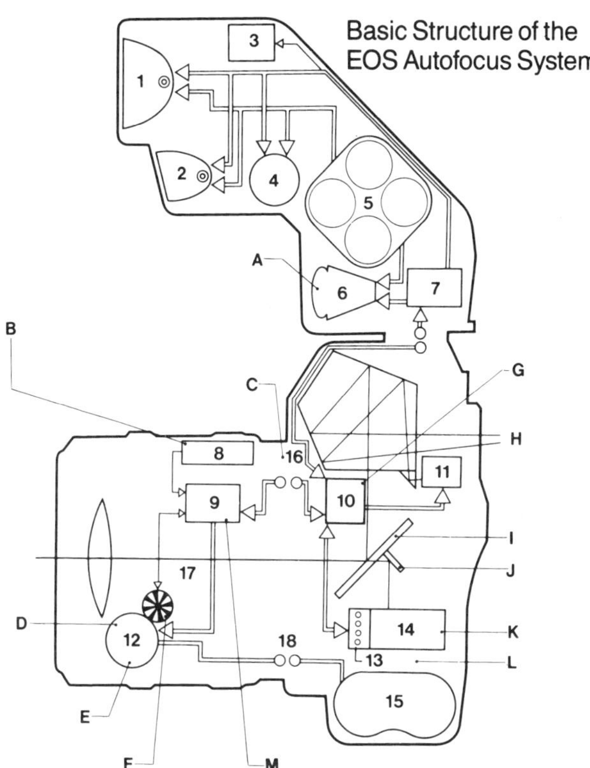

1. Flash reflector
2. Infrared metering flash
3. LCD panel
4. Zoom reflector motor
5. Batteries
6. Infrared metering flash for AF
7. Flash microprocessor
8. Zoom information
9. Lens microprocessor
10. Main microprocessor
11. Display
12. AFD or USM
13. BASIS
14. AF optical system
15. Battery
16. Electronic connection for
    data transfer and power supply
17. Lens position information
18. Power supply

A. Lights for dark, low contrast subjects
B. Focal length information (zoom code)
C. Electronic mount
D. Lens drive motor
E. Ultrasonic lens drive motor
F. Impulse disc (for drive measurement)
G. AF ranging calculation
H. Display of ranging results
I. Full-surface half mirror
J. Auxiliary mirror
K. AF ranging unit
L. AF ranging unit
M. Data transfer and lens control

intensity of the light entering through the lens is measured by a photo diode. This measurement is taken with the aperture fully open to allow the viewfinder image to remain as bright as possible. The camera computer then considers the speed of the lens because the amount of light meeting the photo diode will not be the same with all lenses because of their different speeds. The advantage of TTL metering (through-the-lens) is that, regardless through what lens the subject is metered, the indicated exposure will always consider the lens characteristics.

As soon as you press the release, the exposure will be made and that is that as far as you are concerned, but it is not that simple! First the focal length and speed of the lens are interrogated, the sharpness is measured and stored, and the exposure metered and analysed (multi-field metering). From these values the camera computer will calculate the shutter speed and aperture value and issue camera-shake warnings, if appropriate. When the release is pressed fully down, the mirror is folded away, the aperture is stopped down to the required value, the shutter opens for the calculated period and the film is exposed. The shutter closes again and is brought back to its starting position, the aperture is opened up again, the mirror comes back down and the film is transported to the next frame, everything being fully automatic and motorized. All this takes a fraction of a second and you are then ready for the next shot.

The Eye of the Camera

I have chosen the above title intentionally because it suggests that there are similarities between the human visual organs and the optical system of a camera and

---

Festivals and carnivals are veritable treasure troves for photographers. The 100-300mm zoom is ideal for getting close to people without intruding. In this way you can produce wonderful portraits at a safe distance.

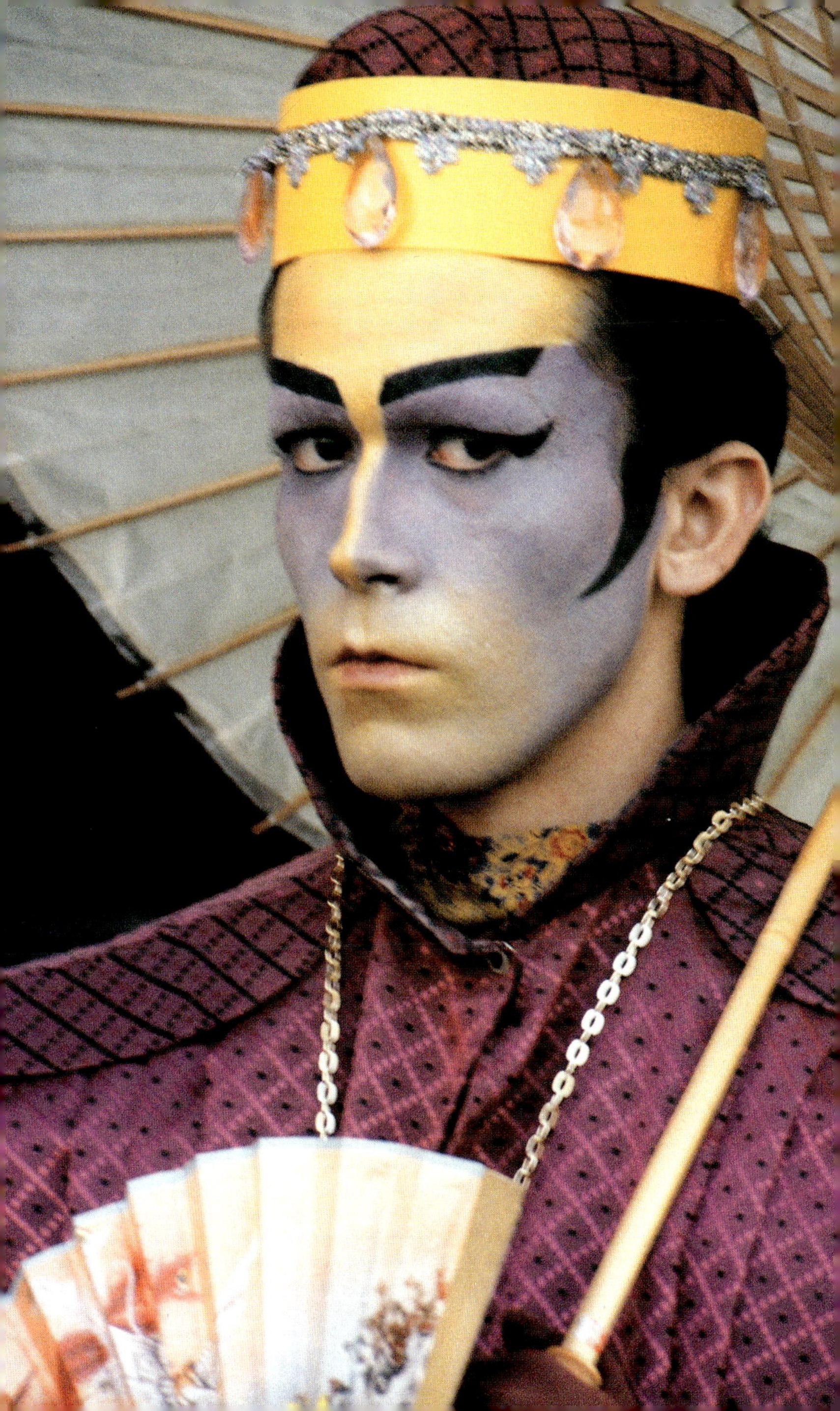

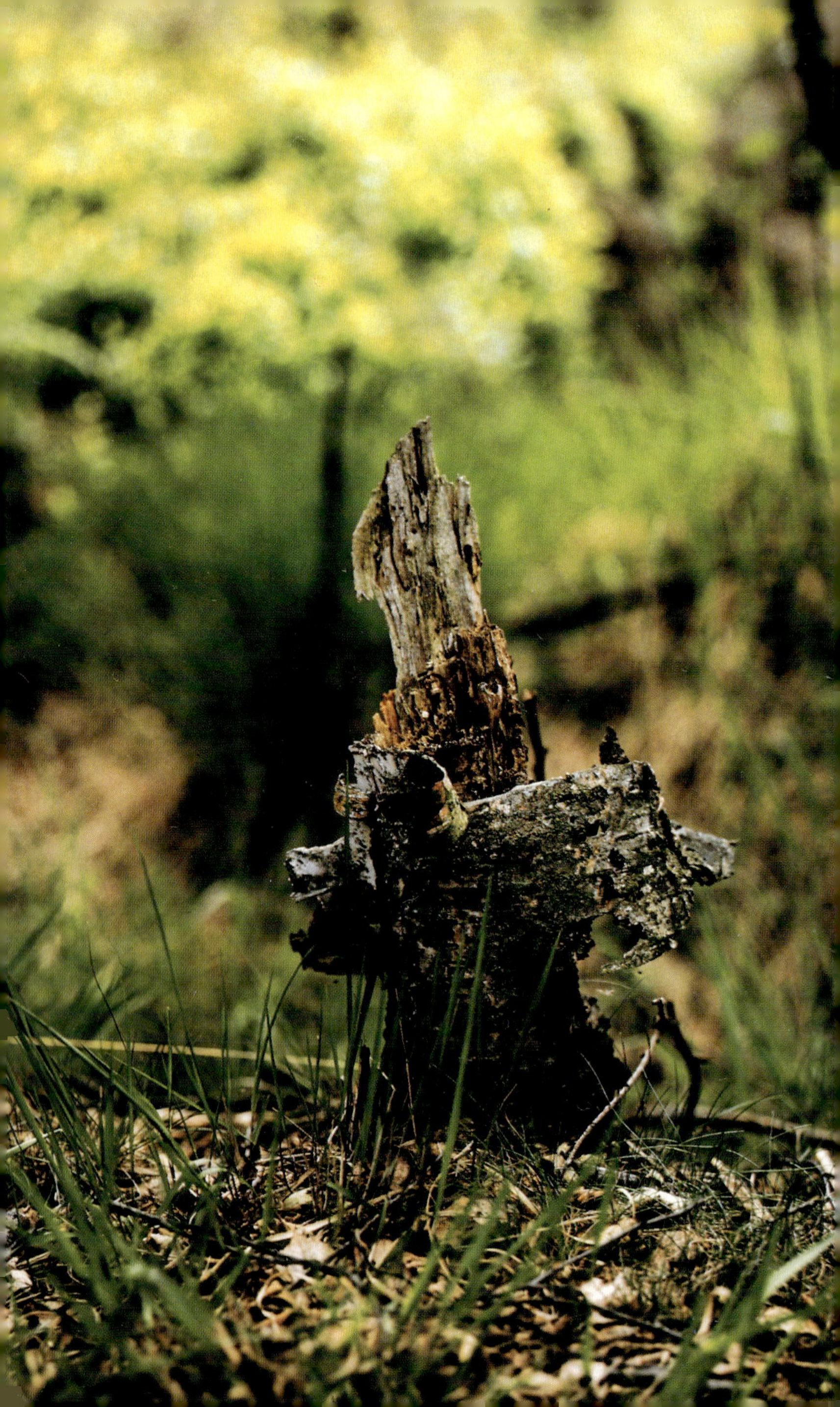

indeed this is so; both produce an image of the surroundings but that is where the similarities end.

The most obvious difference between the eye and the lens lies in the type of image processing. The eye produces an image that is conveyed to the brain via optical nerves. There it is interpreted and assessed as a visual image. Then it is stored away for further reference or is immediately forgotten, depending on its importance. If we talk about the eye we have to keep in mind that it is an organ that supplies information to the brain which decides the importance and meaning of the data.

The film on the other hand, the storage medium of the camera, makes no decision nor does it interpret or order. Whatever is captured by the lens is recorded and never forgotten.

This implies that there are considerable differences between the way the eye and the lens sees because they are formulated in a different way; what we see is not always what is recorded on film. Our eyes are not capable of changing focal lengths but we are capable of concentrating on a particular detail just as you are now concentrating on the written word. However, if you are looking consciously, you will note that, apart from the small area that you see clearly, there is a wider area that is outside your awareness. Moreover, it is easy to change the visual field without having to turn the head. Try to assess the angle of view of the eye; it is almost 180°, allowing for the fact that not everything is in sharp focus. Our eye manages to adjust so quickly to different distances that we are not even aware of it changing focus. The functions of the autofocus in the EOS, on the other hand, are quite noticeable.

It would be quite unreasonable to assume that the eye performs differently when looking through the viewfinder.

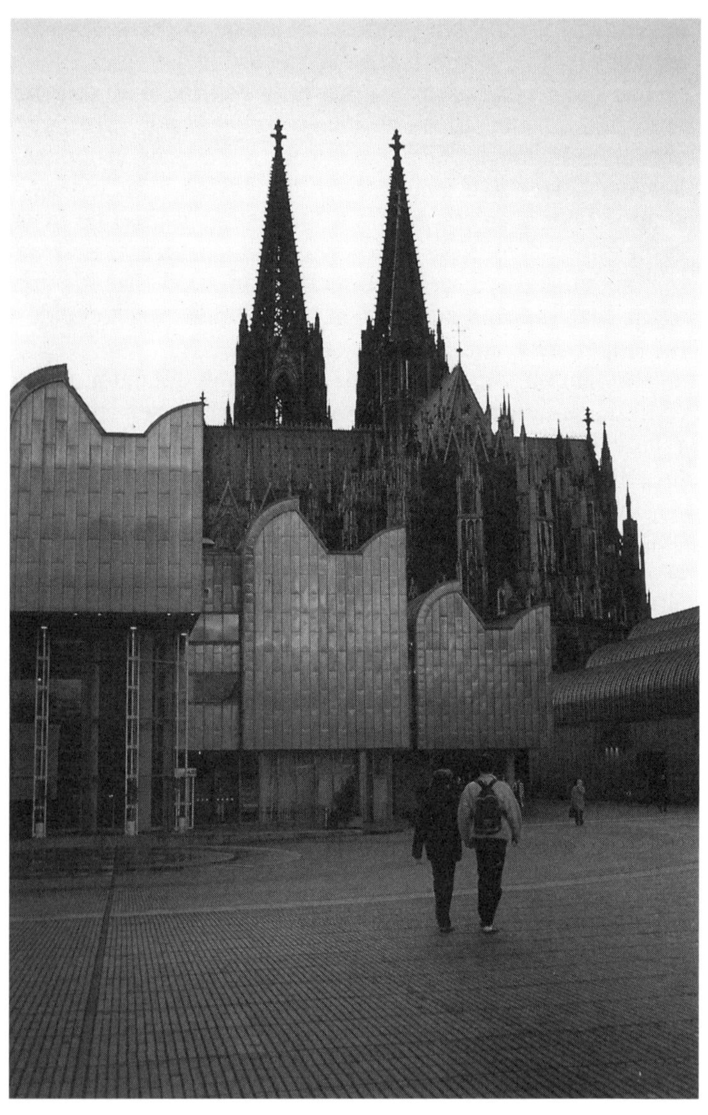

To be able to compose a picture the photographer has to try to "see" like the camera. There are great differences between what we think we see through the viewfinder and what will be captured by the film.

In assessing the image presented, it will, as usual, concentrate on the interesting aspects, suppressing incidental details. Consequently the main subject is often shown, quite small, in the centre of the frame, particularly with inexperienced photographers. Other accidental effects are cut-off legs and arms, protruding limbs, etc. All this is due to the fact that we see only what we want to see.

Then we also have to consider that we have two eyes with which we perceive depth. The image on the film is presented in two dimensions. Information about spatial depth can only be conveyed by the relationship between the objects in a scene.

For these reasons it is a good idea to try and trick your eye by not looking through the viewfinder but onto it. Try to remember that the image in the viewfinder is two-dimensional. Only then will it be possible to assess it properly with respect to impact and composition.

As we have discussed already, the eye is only the conveyor of data to the brain, and we do not see our surroundings the way they really are, but how we wish to see them. You will probably not have noticed that the colours change in your living room at night when the lights are on. But if you take a picture in tungsten light, using ordinary daylight film, then you will be wondering why everything has a distinct yellow hue. "I did not see that" you will be thinking and, indeed, you would not have seen it. You know that one object is red and the other green and you see it as such, regardless of in what light. You don't see the reality, you see what you wish to remember.

The same can be said about brightness. The human eye adjusts quickly to changing conditions. Try and look out of the window and then let your glance wander from the window, across the wall, up to the ceiling and then assess the difference in brightness between the view through the window and the ceiling. The difference will be great but generally speaking we will not notice it. This difference is

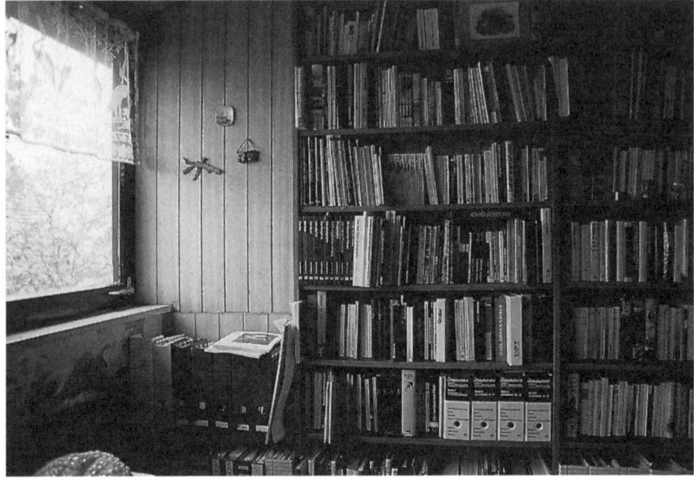

The eye has no difficulty in adjusting between dark and light areas. We are not even aware of how we do this. A film, on the other hand, has only a limited capacity for registering differences in luminance.

easily accommodated by the eye, but a photographic emulsion is not so adaptable. It is capable of showing the window view or the ceiling but not the two together. The difference between the darkest and the brightest area — the contrast — is too great. If the window is correctly exposed the ceiling would be too dark — almost black without any detail. The relatively short exposure that is correct for the window is too short to register any details in the dark areas. If we now expose for the ceiling then the window will be overexposed.

The foregoing example is just one of many where large contrasts present a problem. The backlit shot, for one, is a well-known example. In some situations it is possible to take corrective steps. If the EOS recognises that the subject is backlit it will actuate the flash, provided there is one and it is switched on. In some situations you can influence the exposure reading by selecting a suitable area (remember, the exposure value, which is centre-weighted, is stored together with the focus setting).

116

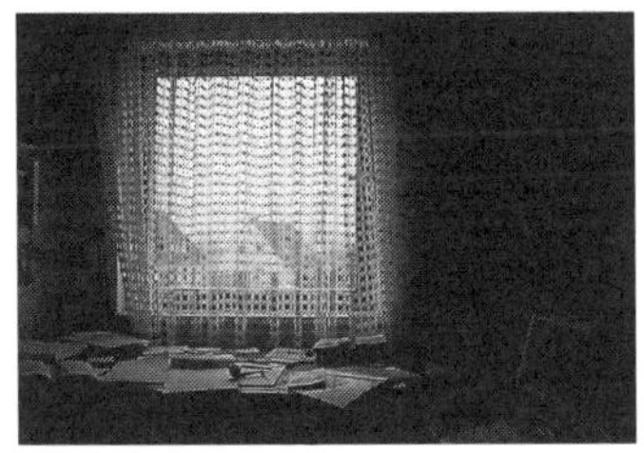 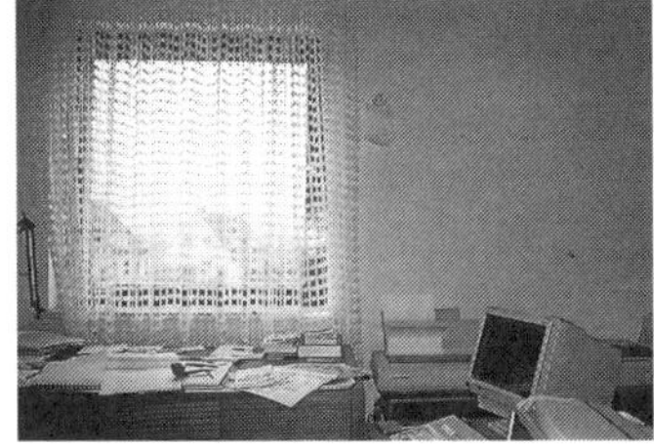

Two similar views of the same subject. The EOS interprets the situation quite differently by slightly changing the metering area. In the picture on the left the central metering area was placed just within the window. In the one on the right, the camera was shifted to cover the edge of the window and the wall. Both are correct, it depends only on how you wish to show it.

It would be a good idea now to take your EOS and point it at the window. Point the AF target field close to the window frame facing outwards. All readings and settings should function normally. Now repeat the process only this time take the reading just inside. Now the autofocus will perhaps not be able to focus and the green **P** in the viewfinder will blink, warning you of insufficient light. If you are using the EOS 750, the flash may be automatically switched on. The lighting situation has hardly changed, the frame has been changed only slightly, but the two situations are interpreted quite differently by the EOS. This implies that the choice of the metering point is the most important decision that the photographer has to make. This choice gets more important when the lighting conditions are extreme.

Playing with Sharpness

Sharpness is important in photography as it is the main aspect of the technical quality of a picture. A sharp photograph is not necessarily a good photograph. An unsharp photograph, on the other hand, is only rarely a good photograph, namely when the unsharpness is clearly an intentional tool to express an idea, or if the subject is

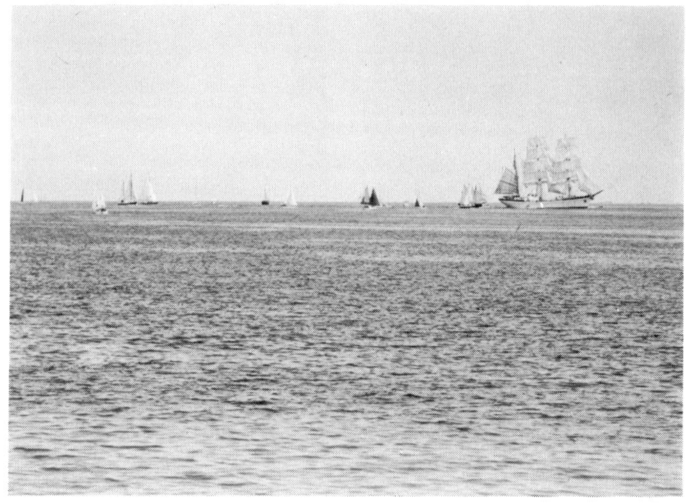
If the camera controls are set for optimum sharpness, then ...

so important that technical quality is of secondary importance. For shots of important events that are still enjoyable to look at after many years, the technical quality is a lesser criterion. Older pictures with faded colours may be of more importance and enjoyment to us than new, technically perfect ones.

The most obvious contribution to sharpness − the focusing of the lens before making the exposure − is performed automatically by the EOS. This is done faster and more precisely than any photographer could achieve manually. The limits and restrictions of automatic focusing have already been discussed.

Apart from sharp focus there are other factors that influence the impression of sharpness in the final photograph. If we look at a large poster from across a street the picture on it will appear perfectly sharp. Move closer to it and the sharpness may seem to diminish and from a very close viewpoint the picture will reveal the individual dots of the printed image and the picture details become unrecognisable. The dot formation is seen only in printed

118

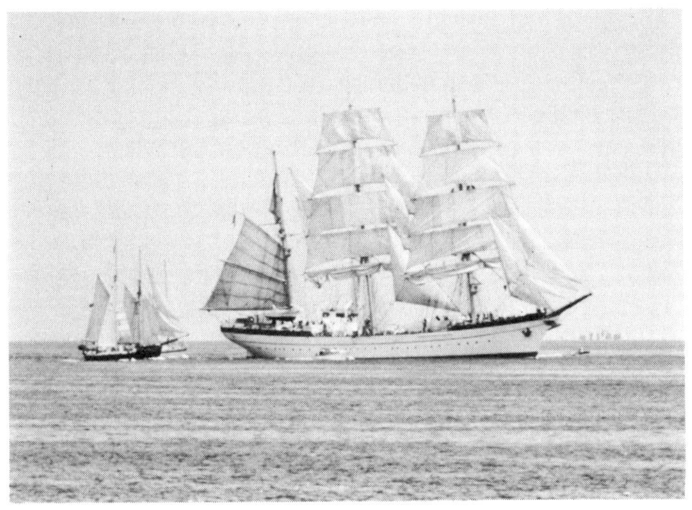

...it is possible to make a selective enlargement, without the viewer knowing that it is not the whole picture. The sharpness here remains acceptable.

images and not in photographs but graininess in a big enlargement can make it look less than sharp when it is looked at closely.

The resolving power of the eyes is limited. An image may look quite sharp from a distance but closer to it may be seen to be unsharp. This happens if a small part of a negative is greatly enlarged and such a picture will appear to be acceptably sharp only at longer viewing distances.

To assess the normal viewing distance for a photograph we use the formula that it equals the length of the diagonal of the picture. Thus a 20x25cm picture can be viewed comfortably from about 32cm. However, in order to view a picture so that it presents natural-looking perspective, the viewing distance should be the product of the focal length of the camera lens and the magnification used in making the print. Therefore a 20x25cm print from a negative made with a 50mm lens, the print magnification being X8, should be viewed from 5 times 8, or 40cm.

But even a picture that appears sharp from a distance

will appear increasingly unsharp as we move closer and we know that our eyes have deceived us. This is quite in order as long as it appears sharp from the normal viewing distance. If not, there is something wrong. This phenomenon can be seen whatever size the photograph.

What are the criteria that determine a sharp impression? The most important factor has been discussed above; the purpose, or in other words, the distance at which the picture is to be viewed. If all you are interested in are postcard-size photographs for your album, then you will not have to worry too much about sharpness. If you intend to enlarge your 35mm negative to poster size then sharpness is of great importance. It is a joy to see a picture enlarged and still remain pin-sharp.

The first decision as to the ultimate sharpness of the picture is made when you load the film. If you remember, I have discussed the dependence of resolving power on the film speed. Faster film speeds require less light for correct exposure whereas slower but finer grained film records more detail. As always in photography, there is a counter argument. The slower the film speed, the longer the exposure time and greater the danger of camera shake blur. There is therefore no strict rule for always choosing slow films because of their high resolution. The film speed always has to be chosen in conjunction with the shooting situation and subject. Slow films are suitable when you are using a tripod, or if you are making copies or composing a still-life. If you wish to capture the fast movements of athletes at a sports event then a fast film is required. In a 9x13cm print you will not even notice that a fast film has been used. However, an enlargement of 20x30cm, say, would reveal the grain that is typical of faster films.

Further factors in the final sharpness of a picture is the camera system as a whole. The performance of the lens with regard to sharpness and contrast plays as much a role as the correct film speed and the reliability of the autofocus function. If you possess a Canon camera you can be assured of the highest standard and it is not very likely that any faults could be attributed to Canon workmanship.

One more word on the topic of lenses. Generally one says that a lens giving high resolution is a good lens but this is only half the story. In addition, edge sharpness or "acutance" must also be good if overall performance is to be satisfactory. It is possible to have a lens with good resolving power that gives indifferent sharpness or a lens that gives sharp pictures but not resolve fine details. Visual sharpness depends very much on the contrast of the images produced by a lens and it is important that fine details should not only be resolved but should show good contrast. A correctly adjusted television receiver can show a picture that appears to be very sharp but the resolving power of the display on the cathode ray tube is always very poor.

Depending on the lens used and the aperture set, the photograph will possess a certain depth of field, i.e. the spatial range within which the subject is depicted in acceptably sharp focus. Because the resolving power of the human eye is also limited we see a certain degree of unsharpness as sharp. In program mode the photographer cannot influence the depth of field and has to hope for the best. If depth of field is important, then you have to switch to **DEPTH** mode. Do not forget when deciding which mode to use, that shallow depth of field can be just as important as great depth of field. A picture that is sharp from close-up to infinity can express one subject perfectly but another subject may be better expressed by a precisely-defined depth of field. Generally one can say that for extreme wide-angle shots, showing a general view, use the largest possible depth of field. The opposite is often true for telephoto shots, where a particular detail is better emphasised against a blurred background. As you can see, unsharpness is not only a problem that has to be limited as much as possible it can also be a creative tool to produce exactly the right effect.

Movement blur, another deviation from sharpness, may also be used as a creative element. There are two types of movement blur. One is called camera shake – movement by the photographer. We all move a little even if we think we are perfectly still. These movements (heart beat, shaking, etc.) are transferred to the camera and the longer the focal length of the lens, the more exaggerated the movement is. This problem is often underestimated. One hears tall stories of how someone took a shot, hand-held, at an eighth of a second. So he may have taken the shot but it is very doubtful if the picture was really sharp. The amount by which it will be enlarged will play a role, of course. A small print may be acceptable but even a moderate enlargement will render this picture useless. I would not wish to suggest that it is wrong to try one's hand even in doubtful situations; who knows, it may come off and the shot be perfectly sharp. Doubtful situation here means about one exposure stop, i.e. one full stop in shutter speed, slower than the limit value. Slower shutter speeds will almost certainly be failures. The golden rule for a safe shutter speed is that it should not be longer than the reciprocal of the focal length in mm of the lens used. In other words 1/focal length in fractions of a second (not 200 seconds but ¹⁄₂₀₀ second for a 200mm lens). In this case ¹⁄₂₀₀ sec is the slowest safe shutter speed for this focal length where a hand-held shot may still be expected to be free of discernible camera-shake. Using a 28mm wide-angle lens, the slowest safe shutter speed would be ¹⁄₃₀ sec. and with a 300mm telephoto lens at least ¹⁄₃₀₀ sec. is needed to stay within safe limits. This rule has been incorporated in the program mode of the EOS and the camera will issue camera-shake warnings if the limit is exceeded.

Nevertheless, keeping within this limit does not always guarantee sharp pictures. If you want to increase your chances of getting a good shot, observe how an expert marksman holds his gun. The same technique can be

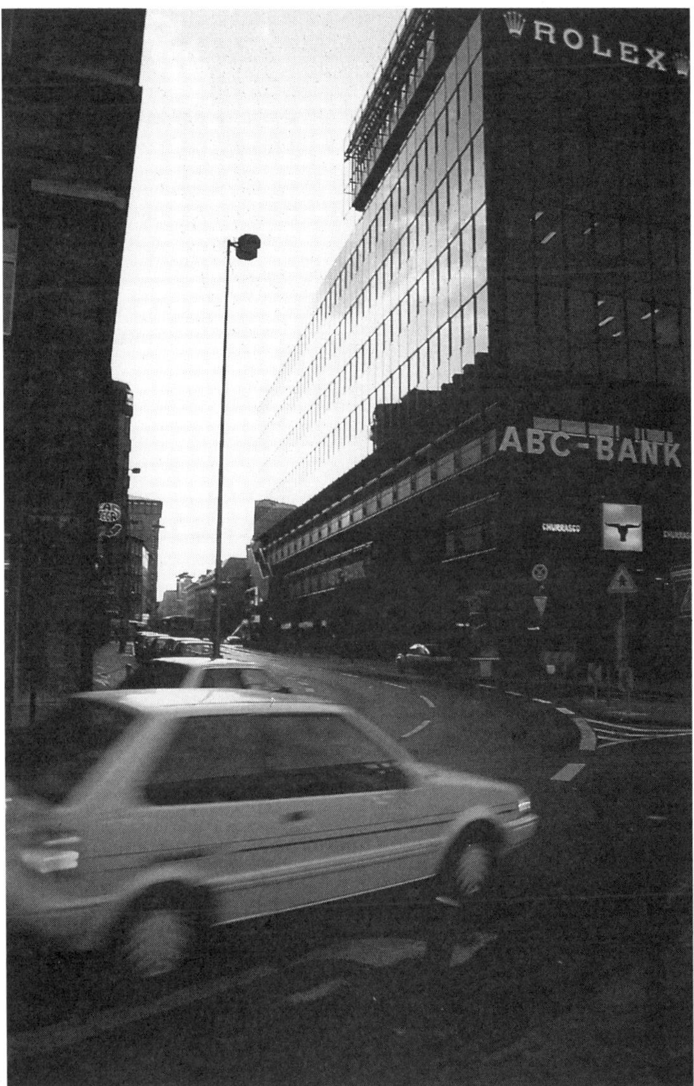

The car is blurred here because the shutter speed was too slow to freeze the movement. To show the car sharply with the EOS 750/850 cameras, you would have to limit the depth of field with a larger aperture, for which the camera will compensate by selecting faster shutter speeds. Alternative: use a faster film.

employed in holding a camera. The ultimate support, essential when shutter speeds become too slow, is a tripod.

Let's assume that you are standing on firm ground. Your camera cradled comfortably and firmly in your hand or mounted on a tripod. Now you want to take the shot. The photographer moves, or sways, and so do subjects. Some may move imperceptibly, like a church spire, others faster, like racing cars. The subject's movement will be shown in the picture as movement blur. If it is a windy day you would experience considerable difficulties in getting a tree sharp in the picture. The branches sway and the leaves are blown to and fro. This type of subject movement may be frozen by choosing a fast film. It would be totally wrong to load a slow film before going to a race meeting. If you wish to be well prepared, take two different films, a slower one for observing the punters, a fast one for the action.

Everything has two sides. The shot with movement blur makes its own powerful statement. It is not always desirable to freeze fast movement; some blurring is often the better way of recording the scene.

Last but not least the subject itself will give its own impression of sharpness. Certain weather conditions, such as fog, haze and drizzle can reduce the impression of sharpness considerably. Then there are other factors such as colour and shape that enhance or reduce the impression of sharpness.

The following table lists the parameters that influence the impression of sharpness of a photograph:

Resulting Impression of Sharpness

Lens sharpness: Influenced by its ability to resolve detail and to show contrast through the size of the aperture and later enlargement

Depth of field: influenced by focal length, aperture, focusing distance and subsequent enlargement

Movement blur: is influenced by shutter speed, focal length of the lens, subject movement and subsequent enlargement

Film sharpness: film speed (= grain of film material and resolution) and subsequent enlargement

Subject sharpness: influenced by form, colour, shooting distance, atmosphere (haze, mist, etc.) and subsequent enlargement

You may have noticed that one factor is contained in all five groups — subsequent enlargement but regardless of which parameter is considered, the ultimate purpose of the picture is the most important criterion in the decision of how much the various factors should be taken into account. After all, to enlarge the whole of a 35mm negative to 20x30cm means that the original 24x36mm = $864mm^2$ is enlarged to 200x300mm = 60000 mm^2. The area is therefore increased by a factor of 69x. This in turn means that the data stored on one square millimetre are magnified 69-times. This little calculation clearly demonstrates the demands on modern film and paper emulsions as well as lens quality. It also demonstrates that the parameters outlined above, which also influence depth of field, have to be properly taken into account to obtain satisfactory results.

In the above considerations the excellent EOS cameras and lenses are the only, admittedly essential, basic premise for success. If we assume that the quality of processing in the lab is good enough you will get good pictures more or less all the time. It is therefore also important to buy a good film and to take care that processing is of a high standard.

It cannot be wrong to always insist on good quality. This does not mean that you should never take a picture just because total success is not absolutely assured. If we restate the parameters that ensure the best possible photos we have: brilliant sunlight in order to be able to use a slow film; a wide-angle lens to make sure that the shutter speed will be within safe limits; absolutely still subjects and a rigid tripod to avoid camera-shake and movement blur. I am sure you will agree with me that the sum total of these requirements does not present a very interesting scenario for creative shots. Generally one can say that it pays to keep in mind all possible causes that could spell failure and keep them under control but don't let them prevent you from taking pictures and lots of them. With luck it may turn out that the totally blurred shot of a windy autumn landscape expresses exactly what you would have never dared to do intentionally.

Films

'A film for my camera, please'.

Unfortunately it is not quite as simple as that. The variety in film material for the 35mm format is tremendous. Colour print film and slide film are available from several manufacturers. The prices vary, some are cheap, some more expensive. The colour characteristics vary from one manufacturer to another; one tends towards blue and is less true in its rendering of the reds, the other is better for greens, etc. Then there are black-and-white films, infrared film, slide copying film, Polaroid film ... Generally, you can't say that one is better than the other, it is just a matter of taste.

The careful shoppers amongst you will first ask 'Do I have to buy the expensive makes or are the products from well-known chain stores just as good, or can I get away with buying cheap special offers?'. Most non-brand films are of very good quality so is it safe to always buy the cheapest? Unfortunately, it is not as easy as that. Research into making film emulsion in recent years has produced considerable progress and the new technology is offered by those manufacturers who are on the forefront of technical advancement. The other manufacturers generally follow the big names fairly quickly but you can never be sure whether the non-brand films offer everything that is currently available.

You can be assured that the film you buy is of the best quality only if it is from a well-known manufacturer. If you consider what particular task a film has to perform the choice will be more difficult. Let me remind you of my example of an enlargement. A whole negative enlarged to 20x30cm means that the information regarding colour, brightness and sharpness stored on one square millimetre of film has to be reproduced exactly at the magnified scale. The best film is just about good enough for this task.

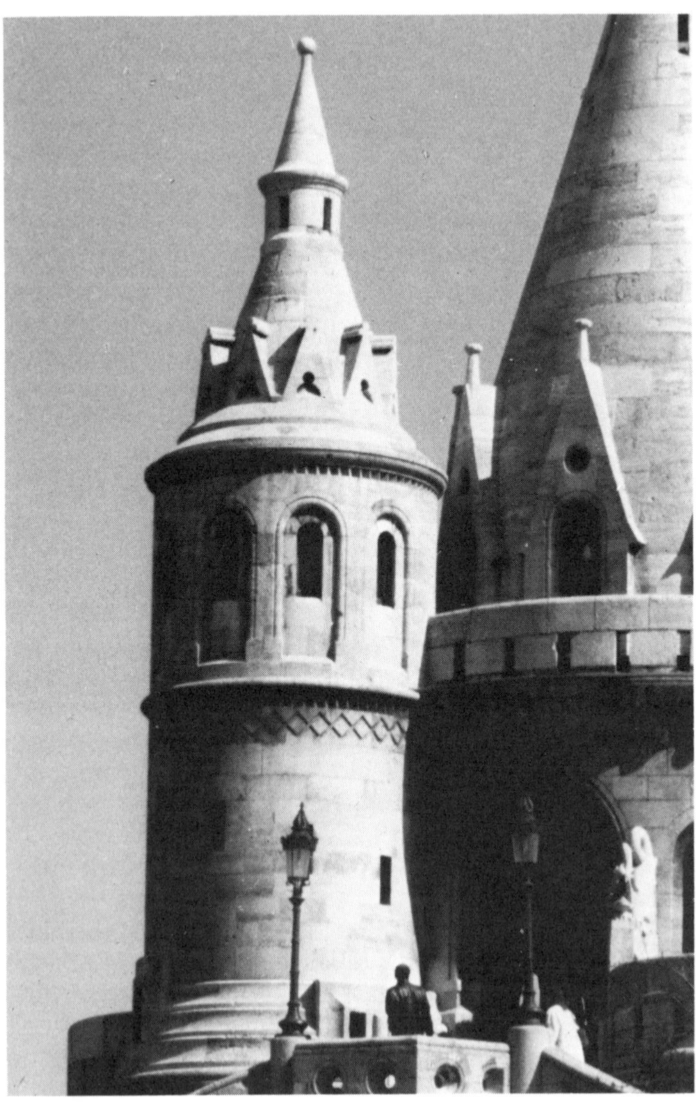

The resolution and sharpness of modern films is excellent but the processing has to be equally good. This picture was taken on Kodak T-Max ISO 100 film. The sectional enlargement corresponds to a 13x enlargement (equivalent to a format of 30x45cm) and is still acceptably sharp.

128

If you pay a little more for your film don't try and economize by taking fewer shots. Better one too many than not enough. The motor in the EOS offers the possibility of taking another shot of the same scene but now the expressions of your models will be relaxed as they are caught off guard. You may find that the first shot is often not the best one. Vary your subject, change your position, move about it to find the best angle.

Film Speed

The film speed stated on the cassette is the most important information − it is the measure of the light required to correctly expose the film. We distinguish between slow, average and fast speed films. The film speed is stated in ISO numbers. This notation is a combination of the former DIN and ASA values. The former ASA 100 or DIN 21 − describing the same film speed − is now called ISO 100/21°. Below is a table of ASA, DIN and ISO values:

Equivalent Film Speeds ASA − DIN − ISO

DIN	ISO
12	12/12°
15	25/15°
18	50/18°
21	100/21°
24	200/24°
27	400/27°
30	800/30°
33	1600/33°
36	3200/36°
39	6400/39°

Following the values down the list, each doubling of the value represents a doubling in film speed. The jump from ISO 50/18° to ISO 100/21° means that the second film is twice as fast as the first. In other words, using the faster film we gain a full aperture stop or a whole shutter speed step, or we can continue taking pictures with the same settings and with only half as much light. If we change from an ISO 100/21° film to an ISO 400/27° film, then we gain two aperture stops, or we can photograph with the same aperture/shutter speed settings in four times less light.

Unfortunately these advantages are bought at a price. The grain of the film increases with its speed. Sharpness and resolution decrease with increasing grain size. Slow films up to ISO 50/18° are very finely grained and have high resolution. These are best suited for very detailed subjects or for big enlargements. Films of average speed are still very finely grained. Film manufacturers have been able to make great improvements in recent years, both in colour and black-and-white film emulsions. For fast films with speeds from ISO 400/27° the grain will be quite visible in enlargements from 20x30cm. However, if lighting conditions are poor, these films will still allow hand-held shots. In particular the new ISO 1000/31° films allow available light shooting which was unthinkable in the past. On the other hand, the large grain and subdued colour rendering can also be advantageously used as a creative medium.

The type of light that the film emulsion reacts to is another aspect of photography. One notable example here is the infrared film. This type of film does not respond to visible light but to a partial range of the infrared spectrum up to about 900 nanometres. Such film is available as black-and-white and reversal colour film and is excellent for experiments. Most lenses have a red dot or a red line, the so-called infrared index. Normal lenses are corrected for colour from blue to red, for wavelengths between 400-700 nanometres (1 nm $= \frac{1}{1,000,000}$mm). Infrared radiation has longer wavelengths and infrared film reacts only to part of the visible spectrum but strongly to infrared. The greatest sensitivity lies at around 800 nanometres. The long infrared rays are differently refracted by the lens and

the focus lies behind the film plane. It is therefore
necessary to shift the focusing to the IR index to obtain
correct focus.

Other unusual films are orthochromatic black-and-white
emulsions which do not react to red. These types of film
are used in photomechanical reproduction and for scientific

Colour and Film

Finally we have to choose between daylight and tungsten
colour slide films. Films are more truthful than our eyes
and brain in the way they see our surroundings. Daylight
is composed of the blue-green-red spectrum with intermediate colours (orange, yellow, etc), each in more or less
the same proportions. When combined, the light appears
white. The relationship of the different colours to each
other is called colour temperature. The lower the temperature (stated in kelvins), the greater is the proportion of
red light, the higher the temperature, the greater the
proportion of blue light. White light has a colour temperature of about 5500 kelvins (sunlight at about midday, with
a clear blue sky), tungsten light around 3200 kelvins
(artificial light) and sky light is about 6000 kelvins or
higher.

A colour sensation is a result of the light reflected by a
certain body. A body that reflects 100 percent of all
incident light appears white, a body that absorbs all the
light appears black to us. If a body reflects only the red
wavelengths we see it as red. An object is therefore not
red or blue but it appears so to us as it reflects only this
part of the visible spectrum. The colour is not a property
of the object; it is a sensation in our brain.

A body can only reflect or absorb the light that it is
exposed to. If the incident light has no red content a red
object will appear black because nothing is reflected.
Tungsten light, for example, has a high proportion of

yellow and red light. For this reason a white object cannot reflect true white light in this illumination, only the red-tinted light and this is what the film will record. Our eyes adapt to this and we don't notice the change in colour. By the way, even natural light changes during the course of the day and with the seasons. We know, however, that a certain object is red and we will always see it as such — the brain converts the "wrong" colours into the "right" colours.

For this reason we can buy professional daylight and tungsten films for colour prints as this film material represents only an intermediate product, contrary to slide film which achieves its correct colours during processing. The colours of colour print film are also developed during processing but they are filtered for any unwanted colour bias during printing.

Lastly we have to consider the reciprocity failure effects for long exposures. So far we have assumed that the same amount of light means the same amount of exposure for the film, regardless of whether the amount of light enters all at once through a large aperture, or a small amount for a long time through a small aperture. This assumption is correct for a wide range of exposure times but for long exposures the reaction of the film emulsion is no longer linear. Doubling the exposure time no longer doubles the effect. For this reason the exposure time will have to be increased beyond the stated length. To state an example of the effect of this phenomenon I shall quote the values for Agfachrome slide film. Between $\frac{1}{1000}$ to 1 sec no correction necessary; from 1 sec, $\frac{1}{2}$ f/stop correction; at 10 sec, $+1$ f/stop. As the reciprocity failure affects the three film emulsions differently, it will be necessary to use colour compensating filters for colour slide film. If you are shooting at night, then it won't make any difference,

---

The exception confirms the rule. In this instance a daylight slide film was used but the subject was illuminated by tungsten light and the effect is a lovely portrait in warm tones.

132

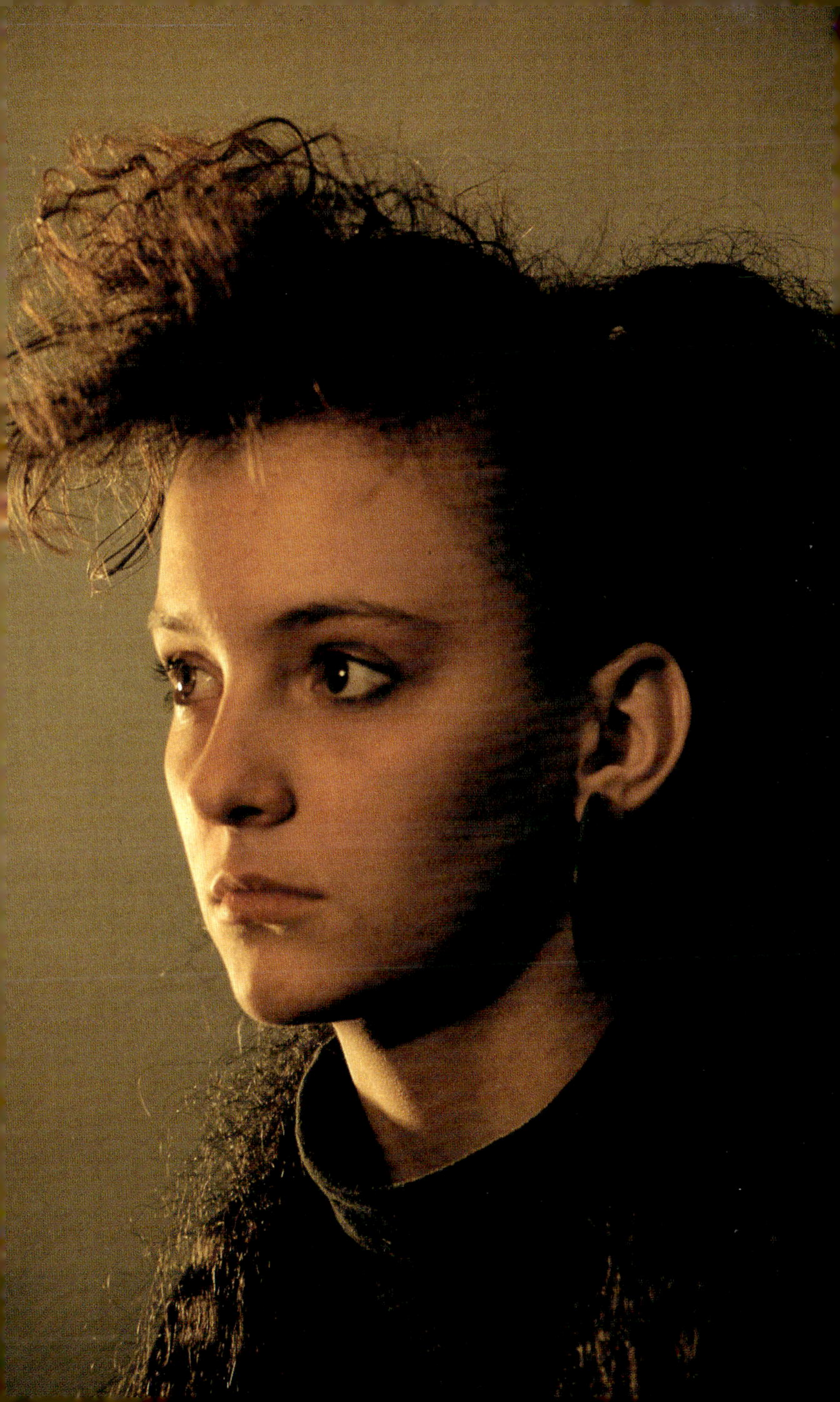

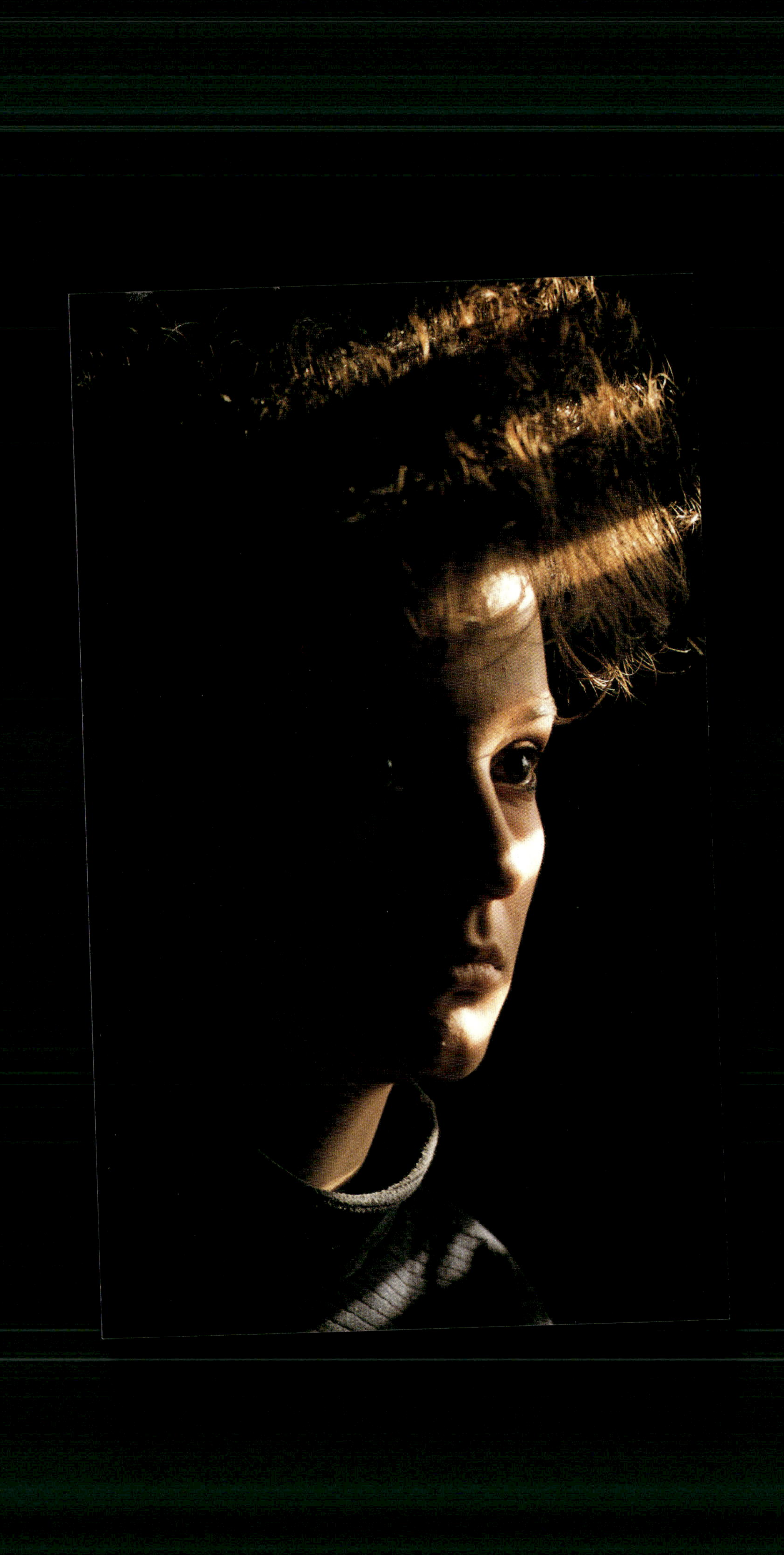

because the available light has little in common with the ideal colour temperature. If you like to give long exposures, then I would recommend that you study the data sheets that are supplied with the film. Modern emulsions, however, are quite capable of accommodating a wide range of exposure times, and long exposures within the automatic range of the EOS (up to 2 sec) should be quite acceptable even without any corrections.

Finally I would also like to point out that there is such a phenomenon as the ultra-short exposure time effect from $\frac{1}{1000}$ sec., which also affects the reproduction of colours.

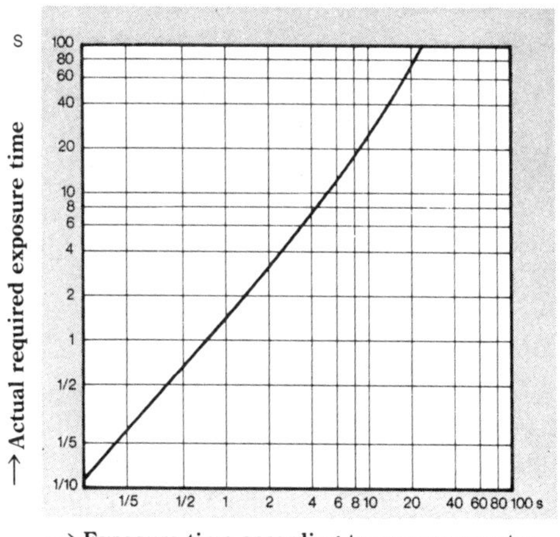

A graph demonstrating typical reciprocity failure. The required corrections are considerable. It is unusual to find data sheets with precise information but this diagram could be used as a general guideline.

Unusual lighting can be used to good effect and the multi-field metering of the EOS copes beautifully.

Slide Film

Perhaps you have already made your choice. If you like to take colour pictures it might be a slide film. This choice is made for good reasons. There is no other medium which produces such reliable results. If you are using good film and send it to a reliable lab you can be sure of good results at any time. As soon as the film is in your hands you can tell with certainty whether your shots were successful — a light box and a good magnifying glass is all you need.

As the slide is already the end product, nothing can go wrong, or be put right, for that matter. Not much can be done if the film was incorrectly exposed, or the frame badly chosen. If you ask your lab to make enlargements from your slides it is possible to choose better framing, or only a section, but incorrect exposure in a slide cannot be rectified. The advantage of a slide is also its disadvantage; after processing it is ready to use — no more corrective measures are necessary or even possible.

For these reasons, slides are best viewed by projection. Unfortunately this is often ridiculed. I know a lot of jokes about photography and the majority deal with boring slide shows. This is often true. What the photographer sees as a really good shot is often quite boring and meaningless to his audience. Friends and relations have to suffer the assault of meaningless shots of the last holiday, of little Johnny, etc. If you do intend to show your photographic exploits, do be critical and restrict the number. Something between 30 and 50 slides are usually sufficient for an evening's entertainment.

Projecting slides by dissolving one into the next is the exception. This method creates a new concept in slide projection. Viewing one slide after the other with a single projector can become quite monotonous, the constant changing from light to dark quite tiring. Superimposition of images by more than one projector adds another dimension. You could also arrange a sound track to

136

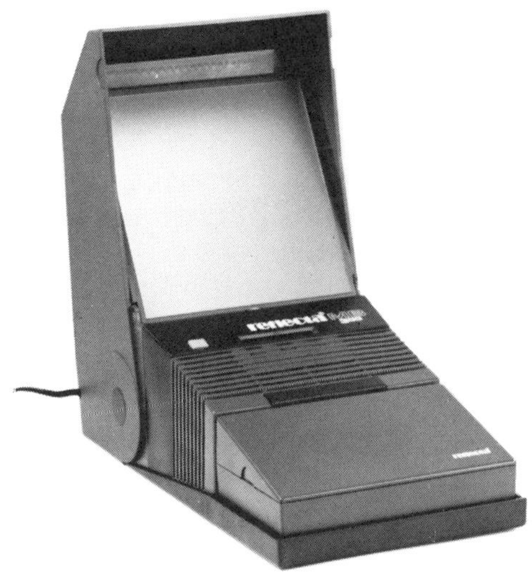

Tabletop slide projectors are a practical way of quickly viewing your slides at a reasonable size and in daylight.

accompany the show.

Superimposing slides becomes another medium, entirely new images can be created, making their own statements. Exciting connections can be formulated, movement can be simulated. You can allow your imagination free reign. The rigid two-dimensional image creates space for imaginary content. The image is no longer fixed, it takes on new forms, a new life, it begins to flow like a film. The creator suggests further images for the viewer.

Slide projection has a disadvantage. Before you can see a slide you have to set up the screen, the projector, and load the slide tray. All this is quite an effort compared with viewing prints. I, for one, belong to those who tend to hold a slide up against the window to see if I have got a suitable shot. Whether they are really sharp or properly composed has to be seen later.

Manufacturers have recognized this problem and now offer table slide projectors. These are ideal for smaller, spontaneous projection. If you want to show a few slides you simply load the slide tray, set the projector up on a table in normal daylight and the show can start. The preparations take very little time and effort and it is almost as easy as handing round your prints. If you cannot afford a large projector you will be well served with one of these portable ones. The projected pictures are large enough to properly assess and view the slides.

I would not recommend doing without screen projection. Only this will really do justice to your best shots, allowing access to a larger public at the same time.

Colour Print Film

A colour print film is more tolerant of under- or overexposure than slide film. A good lab can even manage to print an acceptable picture from a poor negative. Colour prints are very versatile and allow a variety of manipulations but at a price however! The set of prints that you get reasonably cheaply from one of the big processing labs is quite good. Good enough to view and select the best shots. Some negatives may be better than the mass-produced print may suggest. Check with a magnifying glass, perhaps the negative is not as blurred as it looks in the print; perhaps it was just a little carelessness on the part of the operator. Incorrect colour? This too is no reason to doubt your original negative. During automatic processing all negatives are assessed and printed to a general standard formula. If your negative does not conform to this formula, then it may look odd. Of course, the qualities in printers and automatic processes vary but better quality usually means a higher price.

To get the best out of your negatives you would have to print them yourself or take them to a good small lab with your detailed instructions as to framing, colour balance, etc. Only you can know what you intended to express and the effect depends on many factors, not least on the size of the picture when viewed. The larger a

138

photograph, the better its effect. One general rule is that a picture should be viewed from a distance equal to the length of its diagonal. This means that you would have to enlarge all your pictures to at least 18x27cm, as this corresponds to the normal reading distance. Most of us could not afford it. But smaller than 13x19½cm should be the exception rather than the rule. You may have noticed how well this rule is applied when observing a friend as he/she inspects a small picture, because their face moves quite unconsciously closer to it. Apart from the better impression, the larger size will bring out details that you thought were not even captured in the negative.

Black-and-White Films

The question of whether to use colour or black-and-white arises every so often but is really quite illogical. Both media are so different and present no real alternative. There are subjects that work well in black-and-white but are quite wrong in colour. The same holds true the other way round. Many amateur photographers will probably go through personal phases where they favour one or the other, exploring subjects around them, for the ideal expression in colour or black-and-white.

As mentioned previously, to get the best results you would have to develop the film in your own darkroom. This does not apply to slides, but to colour prints and even more so to black-and-white photography. The number of developers alone suggest a wide range of possibilities. If you send the film to the lab, they will simply develop it in a standard formula that is more or less right for every type of film that arrives at their doorstep. Developing at home allows selection of the right type of developer to obtain the best results. So it is possible to develop the negatives to obtain a large grain, or, conversely, as fine a grain as possible. Do not despair at the choice. To start with you may choose a universally suitable developer. After you

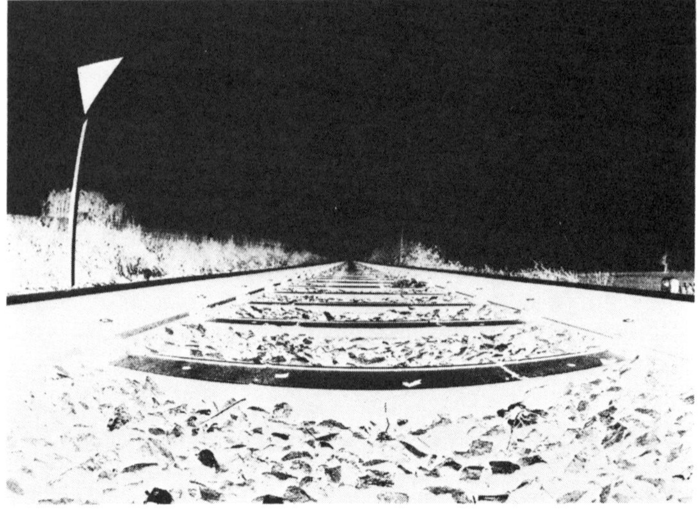

Your own darkroom is invaluable for developing and printing your own pictures and to experiment by creating entirely new images. The above picture is a print from a colour slide where the high contrasts translate into a strange landscape.

have developed and printed a few films you will begin to appreciate what you really want to achieve and how to go about it.

To find a lab to produce good black-and-white enlargements is sometimes difficult. If you consider that the correct exposure of the photographic paper is similar to that of the film, then you will understand that nobody is better equipped than the photographer to know where all the tonal values are to be found. Similar to what I have described under "Practical Photography II" for film exposure, the densities of a picture, and the contrast, can be influenced within certain limits in your own darkroom.

Thankfully the times have gone when suppliers and manufacturers considered black-and-white photography a poor relation. A lot of progress has been made with respect to photographic papers and film emulsions in line with the newest developments in technology. One example is the range of T-Max films by Kodak, which are very

140

finely grained. Only extreme enlargements taken on an
ISO 100/21° negative will show any grain at all.

Polaroid Films

For special tasks you can buy Polaroid 35mm film, both
colour and black-and-white. This is loaded into the EOS
just like any other film. One special feature of this film is
that it can be developed immediately after the last
exposure has been made. These types of Polaroid films
are not for instant pictures as the cassettes hold 24 or 36
exposures. After the last shot it will take only 5 minutes
to process and the finished result can be inspected. Each
film is supplied with the necessary developer.

The quality of these films cannot be compared with
other available films. Their advantage lies in the fact that
they can be immediately developed and inspected. For the
black-and-white photographer there are some special
emulsions on offer which may be of interest. One of them
is the Polablue, a film on a blue base, which will produce
eight slides from black-and-white originals. This can be
useful when producing titles and chapter headings, for
example.

Although Polaroid films are expensive they are sometimes very useful. Because the result can be viewed
immediately they are particularly suitable as teaching aids,
to learn and improve techniques.

Polaroid film costs three to four times as much as
normal film, and you also need a developing device which
costs extra. Developing the exposed film is very easy and
can be performed at room temperature with no necessity
to black-out the room. One thing to remember; Polaroid
film is very delicate and has to be handled carefully. Slides
should be framed as quickly as possible. The framing
accessory, offered by Polaroid, is very handy and used
properly, the slides will be protected against damage.

Practical EOS Photography III – Artificial Light Photography

As the above term indicates, we are talking here of artificial light sources that allow the taking of pictures in the absence of natural light. The EOS 750 and 750 QD have an integrated flash that automatically switches on when conditions demand. Therefore the term artificial light could mean flash but this is only partly true. There are many other, and sometimes better, ways of illuminating a subject. In this chapter I will describe the various light sources that may be used, not only to illuminate the subject, but also whenever light is used as a creative medium.

Flashguns are useful only for general illumination of the subject. With the advent of TTL metering this is usually very accurate, but some disadvantages of flash illumination cannot be avoided. The greatest disadvantage is that one cannot appreciate in advance how much light is reflected from certain surfaces. The small reflector gives a rather hard and direct light which does not enhance the subject. Moreover, it is practically impossible to achieve good modelling with just one light source. The illumination by one direct flash will always be flat.

The indirect flash (only possible with Speedlight 420EZ), bounced from the ceiling, improves matters considerably. However, this creates other problems. The path that the light has to travel to reach the subject and back to the lens is now much longer. If the distance is doubled, the intensity of the illumination is only one quarter even if the reflecting surface is perfectly white. This means that even in a small room, you will soon reach the limits of the output of your flashgun. Also indirect flash cannot be used on coloured walls because anything other

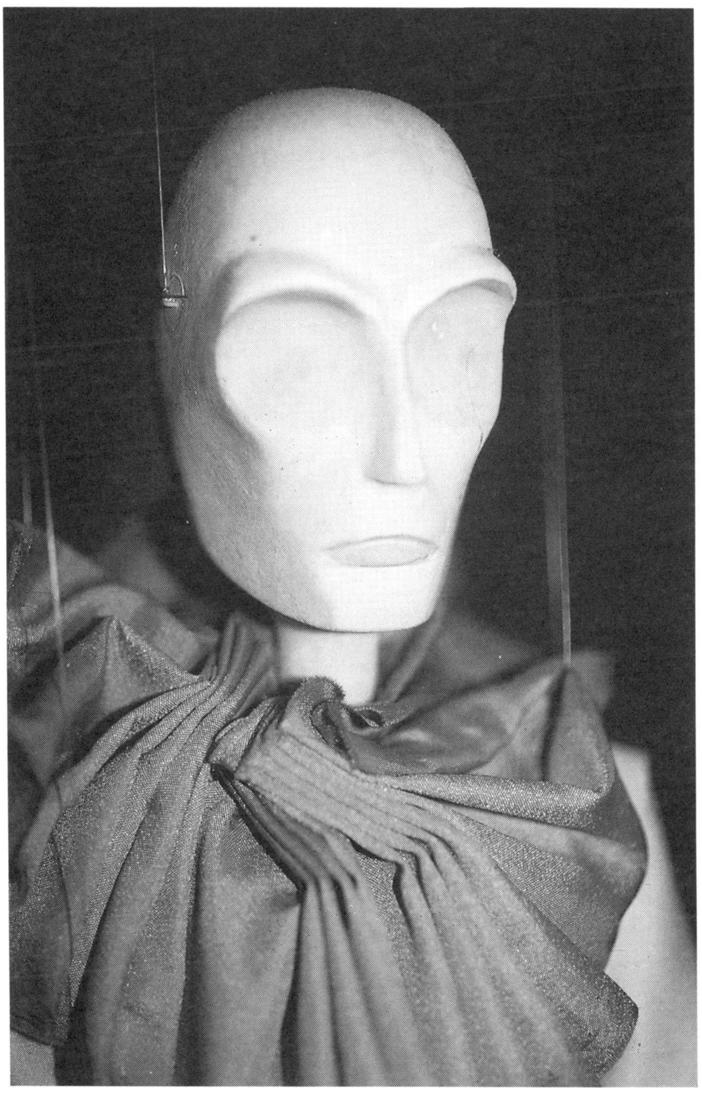

The hard character of flash illumination is demonstrated in this picture. The integrated flash of the EOS lit the subject well but it killed all the subtle tones.

than white surfaces reduce the intensity of the reflected light on the one hand, and on the other, the light reflected back will be coloured resulting in unwanted colour casts.

Flashguns

Even if we take into account all the disadvantages, a flashgun is better than no photograph so every photographer should have one for his camera. It is important, though, not to overestimate its capabilities. Even an expensive flashgun can do no more than supply the same hard light as the integrated flash of the EOS 750, only it will be more powerful. The correct way to use a flash is as an aid for reportage in its widest sense; after all, there are many situations, where a flash is indispensable.

In the case of the EOS cameras it has to be a flashgun that supports all functions to ensure correctly exposed shots. If you are using such a system flash then it will perform the following functions:

○ Setting of the flash synchronization shutter speed.
○ In case of the EOS 750, the release will not trigger until the flash is fully charged.
○ Speedlites: if the flashgun is not sufficiently charged, the camera will automatically give a long exposure as if the flash had not been connected.
○ Automatic fill-in flash for backlit shots.
○ TTL metering of light reflected from the film surface.

When taking flash pictures, the shutter speed must not be faster than a certain value. For the EOS 750/850 models this flash synchronization speed is $\frac{1}{125}$ sec. This ensures that the shutter blinds are fully open when the flash is triggered. The slit will be smaller than the width of the negative with faster speeds, which would expose the frame only partially as the flash illumination time is very short — only a few thousandths of a second. For this reason the flash synchronization time is automatically set by EOS cameras. The exposure is controlled by the flash illumination time and not by the shutter speed. A photo cell measures the light reflected from the film surface and switches the flash off as soon as the measured light is considered sufficient to expose the subject correctly.

The camera computer assesses the results of the multi-field metering system and decides whether the flash should be used for fill-in or for total illumination. The flash has to be switched on, otherwise the camera will make a long exposure with the slowest shutter speed of 2 secs. If the flash is switched on and the section at the centre of the viewfinder is clearly darker than the rest of the subject, the flash will then be activated. In this situation its output will be reduced and the background and foreground will be balanced to show detail in both areas. The aperture and shutter speed are chosen to allow reasonably equal illumination of the foreground, always provided the synchronization time is not exceeded. Whenever there are no distinct contrasts in brightness between fore- and background, the flash is used as general illumination.

Tip: Should you wish to make a long exposure in a dark room and the autofocus is unable to function because of low lighting levels, the small integrated flash of the EOS 750 (or the separate flash for the EOS 850) can assist in the focusing procedure. When the flash is switched on, an infrared pattern, which is used by the camera for focusing, is projected on the subject. After a focus setting has been obtained, keep the release lightly pressed, switch off the flashgun and change the lens to manual focusing. Now you can make the exposure with a slow shutter speed. This is an easy and very convenient way to use automatic focusing even in total darkness or for subjects lacking in contrast.

Canon offer three flashguns. To start with there is the Speedlite 160E, specially designed for the EOS 850. This flashgun offers the same facilities as the integrated flash

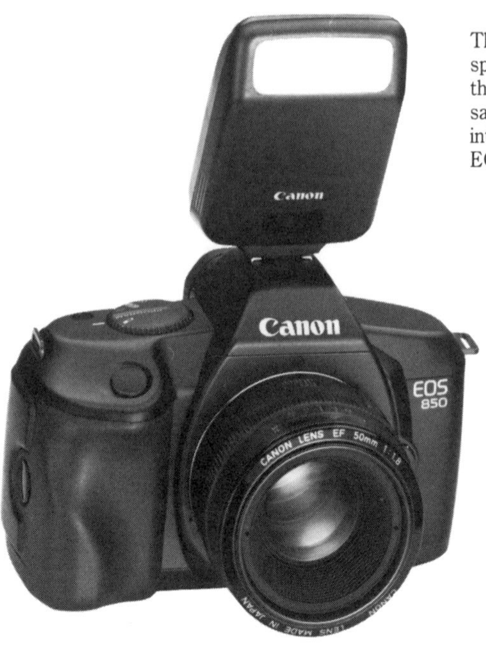

The Speedlite 160E was specially developed for the EOS 850. It has the same functions as the integrated flash of the EOS 750.

of the EOS 750. With a guide number of 12 it is not very powerful, but it is sufficient for fill-in and similar purposes. As the Speedlite 160E is not exactly cheap it is worth considering whether it would not be better to buy one of the EOS 750 models with an integrated flash, in particular as these offer the extra convenience of compactness and automatic activation. Using the 160E is not very different from one of the more powerful flashguns although it is more compact.

Then there are the more powerful variations: the Speedlite 300EZ (guide number 28) and the Speedlite 420EZ (guide number 35). The choice lies mainly in the difference in output. The larger offers 50% more output, which is not a great deal, but its main advantage is the tilting head for indirect flash. Another excellent facility of both these Speedlites is the automatic adjustment of the reflector to suit the focal length of the lens used. Automatic zoom adjustment is possible between 28mm and 85mm. This facility adjusts the output automatically to the angle of view, providing the best possible utilization of flash output.

It is a generally accepted policy of every camera manufacturer to nurture their customers by developing so-called system flashguns. Canon is no exception. Using a system flashgun brings some advantages; automatic change-over of synchronization time, exact exposure metering through the lens, and more. These advantages have to be set against the disadvantages. Such a system flash will not work with any other camera, apart from one of the EOS series, which means that you need a different flashgun for every camera. Moreover, changing cameras will necessitate changing accessories as each manufacturer, and sometimes each camera model, has its own particular accessory shoe, which is not compatible with any other. You are thus stuck with the range of flashguns offered by one manufacturer and have to make do with the facilities offered and pay the price they are asking.

However, the accessory manufacturers soon realized that with the advent of system flashguns, they had to adapt their models to offer the same functions as the manufacturer's own. Unlike the camera manufacturers, the leading flashgun producers agreed on a standard by creating the SCA 300 system, which is offered by companies such as Cullmann, Osram, Metz and Regula. By introducing this intelligent solution they managed to offer the same flashgun for practically all the cameras now on the market. The parts of this system fit so well together that it is no problem at all to combine a flashgun of one company with the adapter of another.

That this solution is much more versatile can be seen by the example of the EOS cameras. The flashguns are equipped with a metering function to allow automatic focusing in total darkness. An infrared flash projects a striped pattern, which is used by the autofocus and although this facility was unknown at the time the SCA

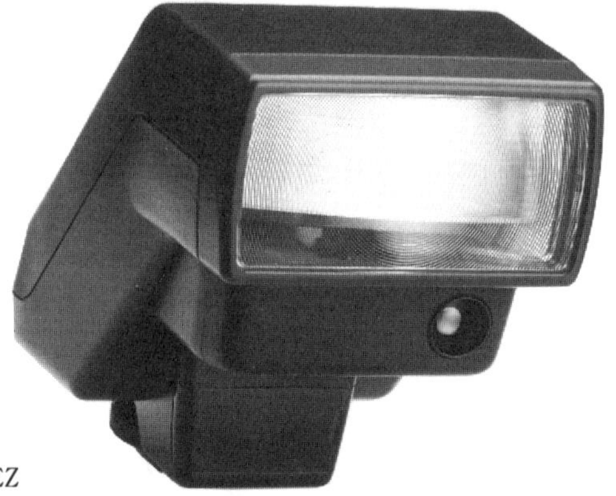

Canon Speedlite 300 EZ

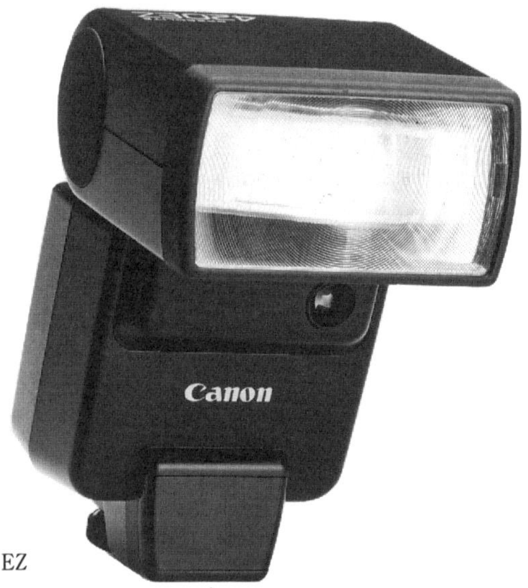

Canon Speedlite 420 EZ

system was developed, there are now adapters available for the EOS cameras with integrated infrared projection!

The underlying idea of this universal system is quite simple. The SCA 300 flashguns provide the whole range of signals. For each camera model a special adapter is developed, which provides contacts for the appropriate

Thanks to the development of the universal SCA 300 system the Canon owner can choose from a wide range of flashguns. Shown here is the adapter and separate flashgun. The necessary signals are monitored from the flashgun and transferred to the camera. The infrared light allows focusing in total darkness. An additional advantage; because of the long extension cable the flash need not be attached to the camera.

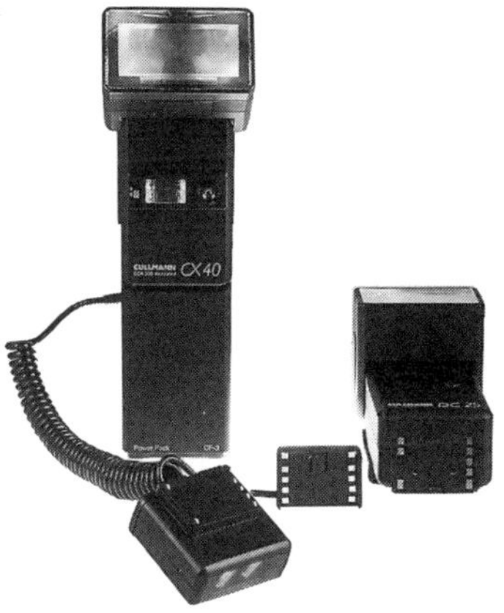

facilities and converts this to a suitable form for a particular camera. In this way it is not necessary to buy a new flashgun, only a new adapter. This offers many advantages to the photographer. He can choose from a wide range, selecting exactly the facilities he wants at a price he can afford, either the system flashguns by Canon or another flashgun with adapter, from the small, handy flash for occasional use, to the heavy duty flash with its own power pack. The system compatibility means you can select exactly the right flashgun for your needs, even if the adapter and the flashgun are offered by different companies.

You should also take into account that the other flashgun manufacturers are more and more inclined to produce specially designed flashguns as alternatives to the camera manufacturer's own system flashguns. As you can see, the choice is getting bigger all the time.

The argument that flashguns by other manufacturers could damage the electronics of the camera is not valid any more. After all, the manufacturers of the SCA system have plenty of experience in the development of flashguns and, as far as compatibility is concerned, they should be equivalent to those offered by Canon.

Canon system flash, yes or no? So you ask whether you should buy a Canon flashgun or another make. There is one advantage that another make does not offer, the automatic zoom reflector. For this reason I would recommend one of the Canon flashguns with higher output. The two more powerful Speedlites maintain the basic philosophy of automatically performing all the complicated tasks for the photographer. In special cases other makes of flashguns could be better − if you are considering a particularly tempting special offer or if you need a very powerful flashgun, perhaps with an additional power pack. After all, one can buy flashguns with output ratings up to a guide number of 60, which is almost four times the output of the Speedlite 420EZ (doubling of the guide number corresponds to a quadrupling of the flash output!).

Tips/Conclusions

○ Flashguns are handy to carry around and provide sufficient illumination for almost every situation and shooting distances up to 10 metres.
○ The **DEPTH** mode cannot be used with flash.
○ The light is rather hard so take care of heavy shadows. It is difficult to model the subject as the flash just lights up the surfaces that face the camera.
○ The effect of the illumination cannot be controlled.
○ Flashguns are useful for photo reportage − to show an event, who was there and what happened.
○ The flashguns available for the EOS cameras are not suitable for shots where the subject needs to be illuminated in a controlled way for specific effects, unless the hard light is intentional for creating a dramatic effect.

Rechargeable or Ordinary Batteries?

Flashguns consume considerable battery power. If you use flash a lot, the cost in batteries can be considerable. The disposal of exhausted batteries is another problem. These, including lithium batteries of the type used by the EOS, are highly toxic and should be disposed of by returning them to a dealer. Rechargeable batteries can be considered environmentally safe. They can be used over and over again, up to thousand times, so the ratio of energy to raw materials is high, as only one cell is used instead of several hundred.

If you use your flash only occasionally, ordinary alkaline batteries are the most convenient way of powering it. Rechargeable batteries are more expensive and you also need a charger. I therefore suggest you start with ordinary batteries until you can assess how much power you need and whether it is worth investing in chargeable nickel cadmium cells.

If you have to change your batteries more often than two or three times a year, then it may be worthwhile investing in a set of rechargeable nickel cadmium batteries and a charger. There is an additional advantage; the flashing rate for rechargeable batteries is higher; however, the number of flashes per charge is reduced but this should present no problem as the battery can be recharged at negligible cost.

Tip: Always keep a set of spare batteries in your gadget bag; nothing is more annoying than running out of power at the wrong time.

Studio Photography

The term Artificial Light Photography also covers the well-considered use of light as a creative medium. Usually

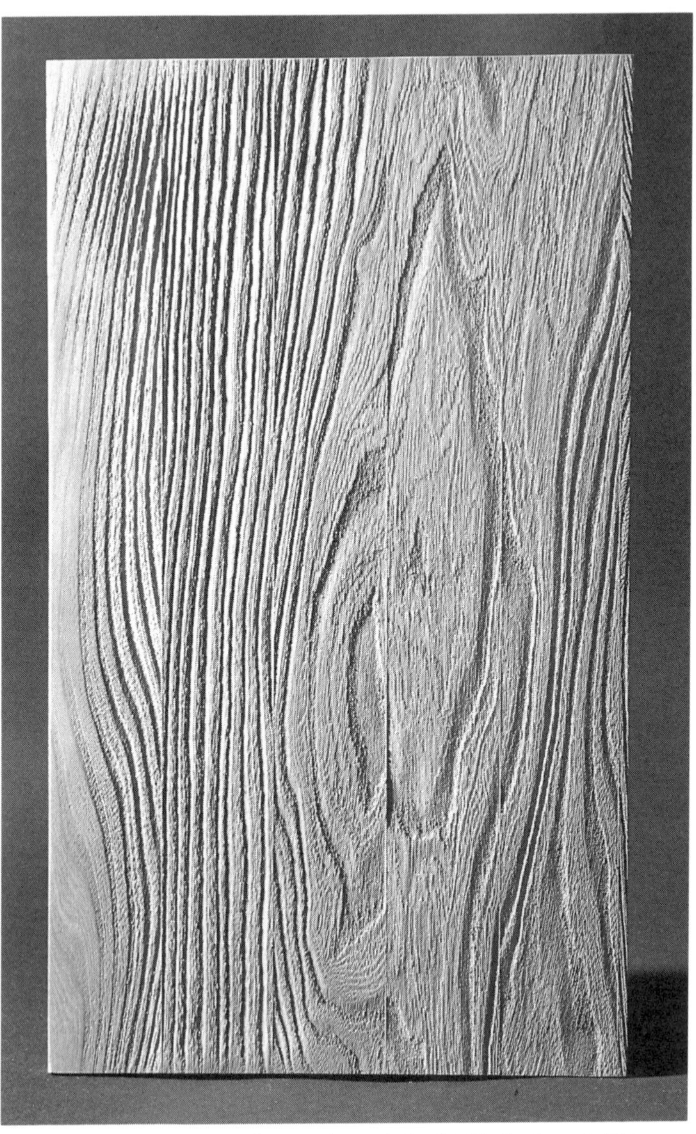

Side lighting was used to bring out the grain in this block of wood. This can easily be achieved with studio lights. A flash pointing directly at the subject would have destroyed this effect.

you need more than one light source — main light, fill-in light, spotlight, background light, etc. The situation here is that the light can be controlled by various means such as screens and reflectors.

In this connection I would like to say that although the EOS 750/850 is a good and uncomplicated camera it does have its limitations. Artificial light photography is one example. As it is not possible manually to preselect the aperture, the exposure also has to be controlled by the camera. This implies the use of a system flashgun with the loss of the **DEPTH** program mode and consequently no control over depth of field. Unfortunately, we have to accept this.

The term "studio photography" conjures up visions of professional photographers manipulating expensive equipment, such as flash generators of enormous output, with prices to match. But not only the professional, the amateur photographer also wishes to be independent of the changing conditions of daylight and to exert a measure of control over them. However, only few of us will be able to afford to furnish a room with this type of equipment. I can only advise you to clear a corner of a room now and then and to experiment under controlled conditions. You should still be able to produce reasonable portraits, still-life and tabletop photography. The most important element in this type of photography is the lighting. This should be totally controllable and as versatile as possible.

Here, this term means taking photographs under controlled conditions where the photographer is able to determine all parameters from film speed to illumination. In this case low speed films are preferred, producing very sharp pictures with very fine grain. The illumination can be soft to flatter or hard for dramatic effects.

This does not mean that daylight is always unsuitable. Quite the contrary is true at times. Many subjects benefit greatly by the mood and tonal qualities that only daylight produces. Any type of natural light, from the brightest direct sunlight to moonlight, provides the widest range of expressions. The type and mood of the lighting is therefore the decisive factor in any photograph. Almost any type of light is suitable, as long as it is used for the right subject, to express its particular characteristics to full advantage.

On the other hand, there are situations where the light is not the decisive factor and may not be suitable or controllable for the intended purpose. For example, the subject could be located in the foreground, such as for portraits or still-life. In these situations it is desirable to be able to control the effect and colour of the light before taking the shot.

Normal flash has the disadvantage that it can't be exactly assessed so it is impossible to achieve precise modelling effects. The following situation describes a set-up which offers these facilities. I am talking about studio lights, using normal tungsten light. The only difference from domestic light bulbs is that this equipment uses bulbs rated from 250 to 1000 watts. The light can be directed by various types of reflectors to illuminate a selected subject area. Another important advantage is that the light sources are independent of the camera and can be placed anywhere around the subject. You can experiment with main light, top light, side light, etc. More than one light source can be used to show the subject to full advantage. Position your lights and your subject, and set the camera to program mode. Be careful to check that the flash is switched off. Another consideration; if you are working with slide film, make sure you are using a tungsten film or daylight balanced film with a blue conversion filter. The **DEPTH** program should be particularly suitable in this situation for exact control of depth of field.

Studio lights are not exactly cheap. To invest in such a

An example of how a small studio with just two lights can be very effective in producing good figure studies.

154

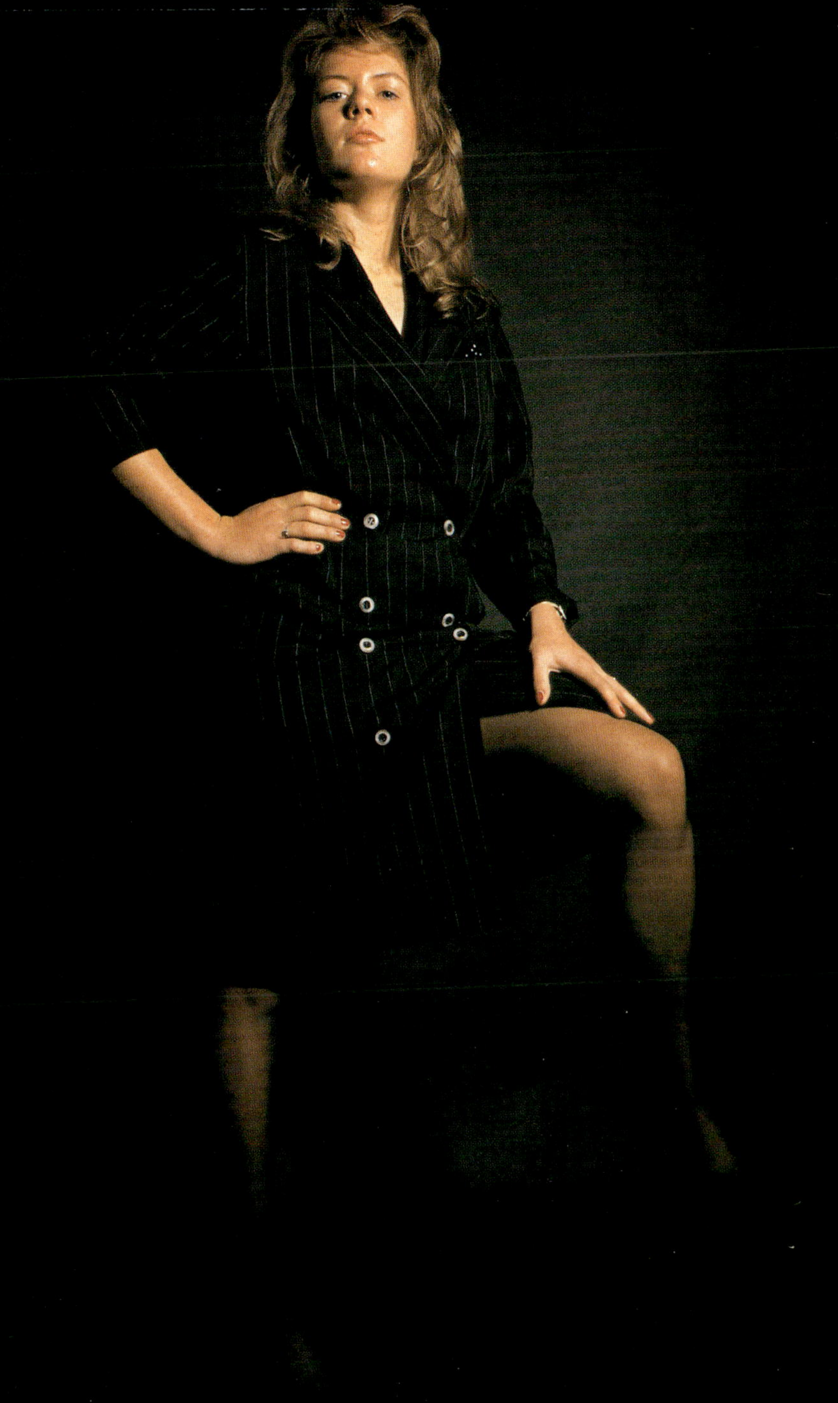

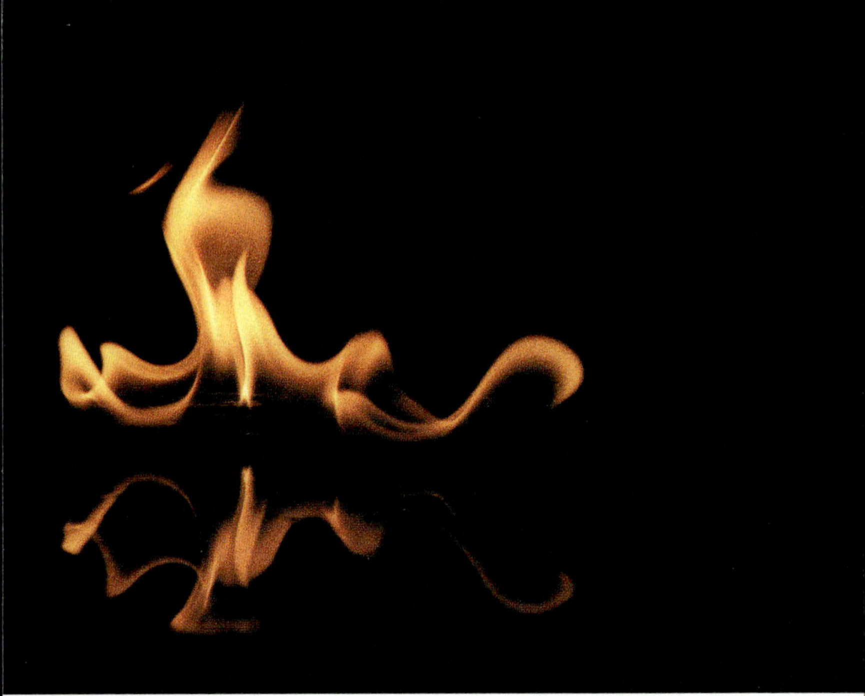

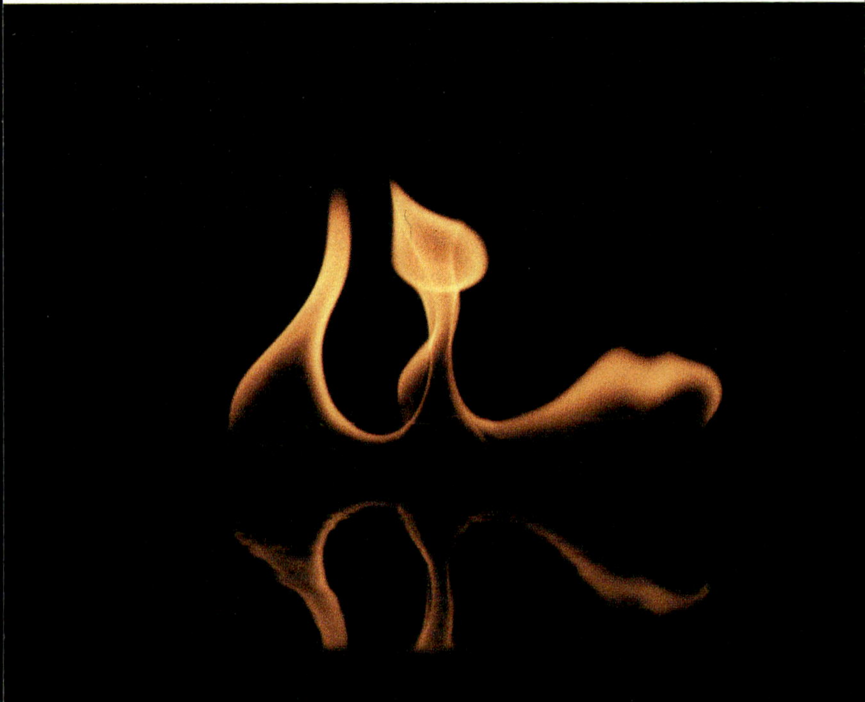

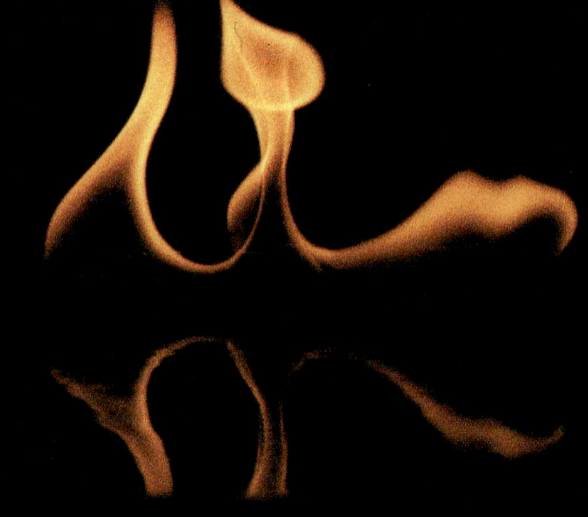

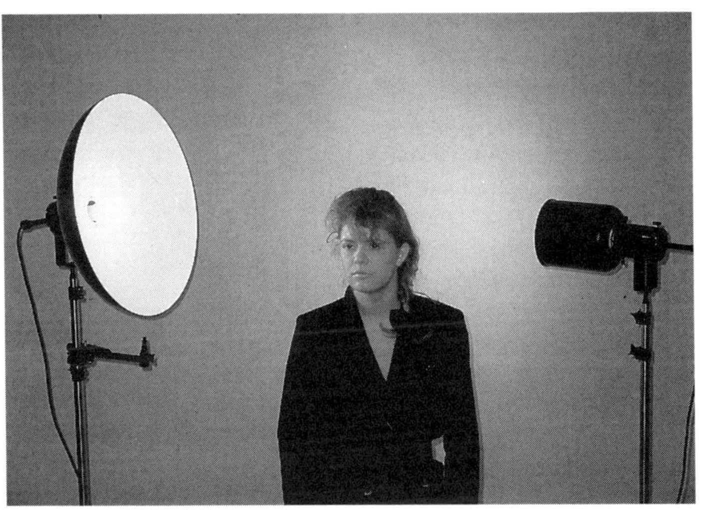

Studio lights allow imaginative illumination of the subject. Each light would cost about as much as a flashgun. Various reflectors and screens help to control the light to produce a precisely-controlled effect.

home studio is worthwhile only if you are particularly interested in this type of photography. Before you go and spend a lot of money, why don't you try it out with a few spotlight lamps that may be available at home? The results may not be perfect but you will get some idea of how it's done.

Some special photographic lamps have an integrated reflector and may therefore seem a good buy. This is true but they are less suited for modelling purposes as the light can neither be directed in a narrow beam nor can it be diffused, but here too, quite suitable for initial experiments. When trying to use normal domestic lamps take care not to overload the equipment. Most domestic lampholders are not designed for high wattages such as 500W.

Knowing how – this is the most important factor in photography. These effective studies were produced by igniting a little lighter fuel floating in a small dish of water, the shot being taken against a black background.

If you want to try out artificial light photography I would recommend the following; use either Ektachrome tungsten film rated at ISO 50/18° or use colour negative or black-and-white film. Now you can experiment with as many lights as you can find or consider useful, positioning them at different distances and angles. The EOS will make your exposures in the program or **DEPTH** mode and you should be able to assess the effect of the lighting even before the shutter is released.

If you enjoyed this experiment then you may decide to invest in your own studio equipment. To start with you will need two lights, with reflectors, one with a narrow beam and the other giving diffuse light and perhaps one or two reflecting screens. This gives a variety of combinations with just two light sources.

Tips/Conclusion
○ If you are working with slide film, use tungsten film, or daylight film in conjunction with a conversion filter.
○ The **DEPTH** program is suitable.
○ Take your time; take several pictures, varying the positions of the subject and lights, change the focal length and the depth of field, and why not try a black-and-white film?
○ Experiment with the lights. Taking notes may help. The effect on the final photograph is often different from what is seen.
○ First set up the main light, then the fill-in lights, otherwise the illumination may be flat and uninteresting.
○ It is not always necessary to use several light sources, sometimes just one light and a sheet reflector is exactly right.
○ A slide projector is excellent as a spotlight or for an unusual background.

Made To Measure

The EOS models are comprehensively equipped. Canon's motto being all the essentials without any unnecessary gimmicks. The eyecup, for example, has been attached to the viewfinder as standard.

Indeed, it is possible to simply pick up an EOS 750 or 850 camera, and − whatever the situation − take good pictures. Still, there are a few accessories that come in handy at times and I have devoted the next few pages to some for use with the EOS cameras. Furthermore, I have also included some matters to consider when building up a photographic outfit.

Accessories

Lens hoods: These are available in metal or plastic. They keep stray light out of the lens as this causes unwanted reflections, which reduce the brilliance of the pictures.

You should have a hood for every lens. Even if it is not always absolutely essential, it can never do any harm. Personally I prefer the flexible rubber or plastic ones as these can be folded back and kept on the lens at all times.

In the case of zoom lenses the use of a hood is a little more difficult. Care must be taken that the hood does not cover part of the frame because the one suitable for the longer focal length settings towards 70mm will act as a vignette if the zoom is set to 28mm, because of the increased angle of view.

If you use a lens hood with a zoom lens, then it has to be one that is suitable for the shorter focal length settings of the zoom. It will no longer be effective for the longer focal length settings but at least the shorter focal lengths are suitably protected. For the longer settings you could hold up your hand against the sun, but care is needed so

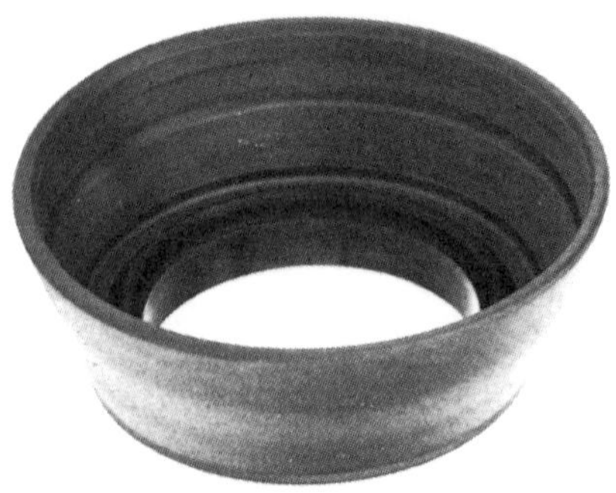

Every lens should be fitted with a hood. Please note however that the front element of some Canon zoom lenses moves when the focal length is adjusted.

that it is not included in the picture.

It is possible to obtain adjustable lens hoods, Whether these are practical is doubtful. There is always the danger that you forget to adjust it and the pictures in a very important series are all vignetted. The best solution would be an integrated lens hood, that is automatically adjusted with the changing focal length!

With some zooms the front element moves when the focal length is changed. This means that the filter thread will also move in or out of the lens tube. An attached hood could impede the adjustment of the focal length.

Carrying strap: This simple accessory can be quite useful. Whether you wish to buy another type of strap depends on how you carry the camera.

Some photographers carry their camera around their neck, lifting it to their eye, whenever a scene seems interesting. This is very convenient as the camera is always secured against loss or accidental dropping. The carrying strap supplied with the camera should be very useful for this type of shooting/carrying. Be careful, though, that you have secured the strap properly as it is not always as easy as it seems at first glance.

If you like to work sometimes with, sometimes without, the carrying strap, then you might favour a quick release hook. There are many interesting variations on the market and you might find a suitable strap that can be easily released and re-attached. Buy a wide carrying strap as this is more comfortable on a long trip.

If you don't need the original strap any more, don't forget to save the little eyepiece cover which is kept in the anti-slip section of the strap. This has to be attached to the eyepiece when making long exposures to prevent light entering the viewfinder, which could confuse the metering.

Eyesight correction lenses: Canon offer ten different dioptre correction lenses which are simply attached to the eyepiece. These lenses will correct short and long-sightedness in the range of −4 to +3 dioptres. Most find it easier to inspect the viewfinder image without glasses as the eye is closer to the eyepiece and the framing and viewfinder displays can be better assessed this way.

Gadget Bag: This is the most important accessory that no photographer should be without. A good quality camera bag will usually be the best. To invest in an aluminium case makes sense only if your equipment is exposed to extreme stress or if you intend to go on safari or shoot in the tropics. A soft camera bag is usually better for general use as it is not so heavy and therefore easier to carry.

The range of camera bags on offer is vast, and every taste and need seems to be catered for. There are several points to be considered when deciding on a bag. First of all it has to be big enough to accommodate the camera plus all accessories. A little bigger than absolutely necessary may be a good idea, just in case you do buy one or two more lenses, or a flashgun. Make sure that all zip fasteners, etc. have covers to ensure that the openings are waterproof. It may be too much to ask for a completely waterproof bag, but a good one should afford protection against a heavy shower of rain. The bottom of the bag should have some stiffening so that it can be carried comfortably even with some heavy equipment, because a

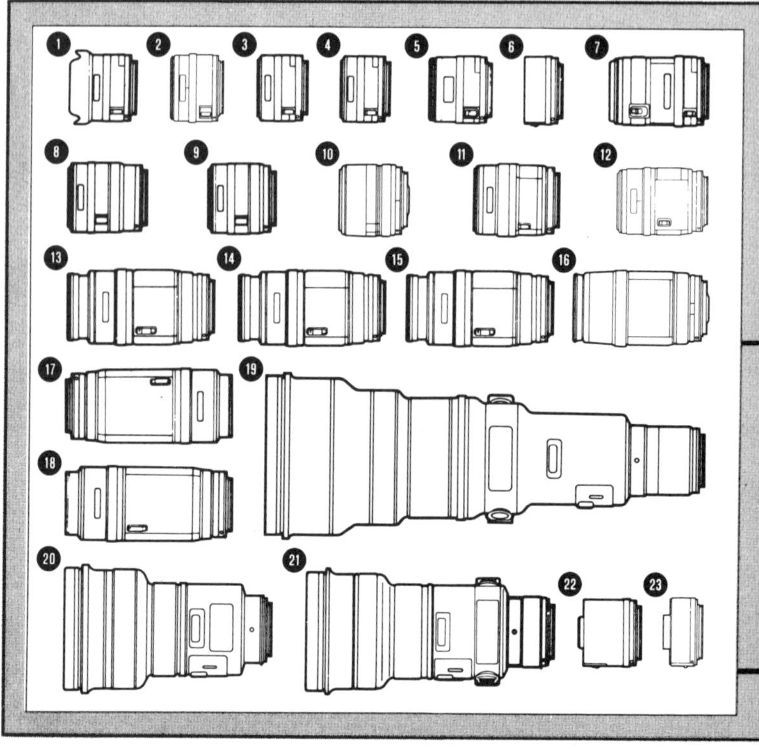

An overview of the EOS system. Please note that not all the accessories are compatible with every camera in the system. Interchangeable focusing screens, data backs and the remote release can be used only with the 600 (630), 620 and 650 models.

1. EF Fisheye 15mm, f/2.8
2. EF 24mm, f/2.8
3. EF 28mm, f/2.8
4. EF 50mm, f/1.8
5. Compact macro EF 50mm, f/2.5
6. Life-Size Converter EF
7. Soft focus EF 135mm, f/2.8
8. EF 28-70mm, f/3.5-4.5
9. EF 35-70mm, f/3.5-4.5
10. EF 35-70mm, f/3.5-4.5 A
12. EF 35-105mm, f/3.5-4.5
13. EF 50-200mm, f/3.5-4.5

14. EF 50-200mm, f/3.5-4.5 L
15. EF 70-210mm, f/4.0
16. EF 100-200mm, f/4.5 A
17. EF 100-300mm, f/5.6
18. EF 100-300mm, f/5.6 A
19. EF 600mm, f/4.0
20. EF 200mm, f/1.8 L
21. EF 300mm, f/2.8 L
22. Extender EF 2X
23. Extender 1.4X
24. Speedlite 160E
25. Speedlite 420EZ
26. Speedlite 300EZ

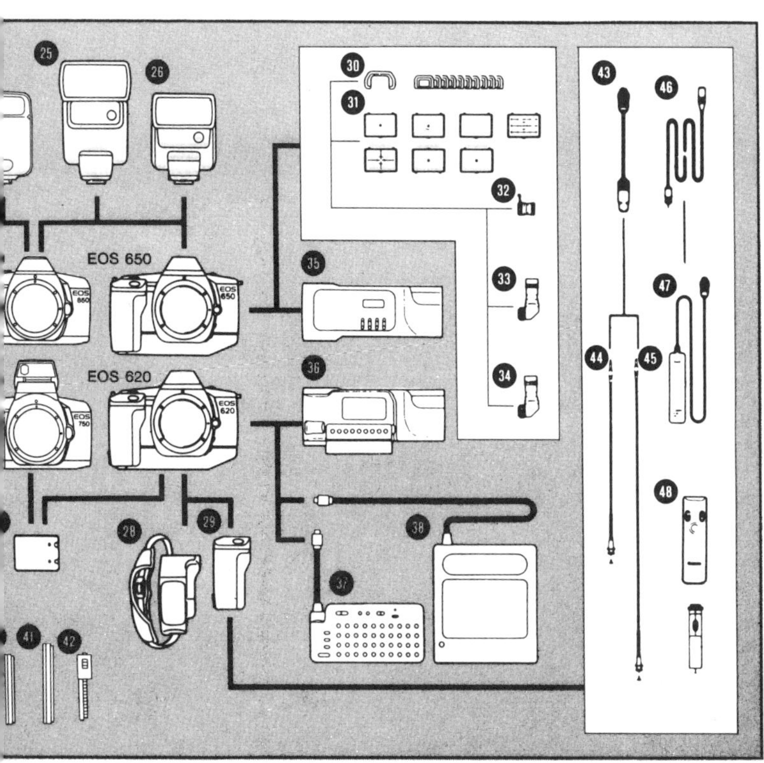

27. Lithium battery pack
28. Handgrip GR10 (Grip L)
29. Handgrip GR20
30. Rubber eyecup/Eyesight correction lenses
31. Focusing screens E
32 Magnifier S
33. Angle Finder A2
34. Angle Finder B
35. Quartz Data Back E
36. Technical Back E
37. Keyboard Unit E

38. Interface Unit TB
39. Circular Polarising Filter PL-C (dia 52mm)
40. Circular Polarising Filter PL-C (dia 58mm)
41. Circular Polarising Filter PL-C (dia 72mm)
42. Circular Polarising Filter PL-C (dia 48mm, drop-in type)
43. Cable Release Adapter T3
44. Release 30
45. Release 50
46. Extension Cord 1000T3
47. Remote Switch 60T3
48. Infrared Remote Control LC-2 Set

163

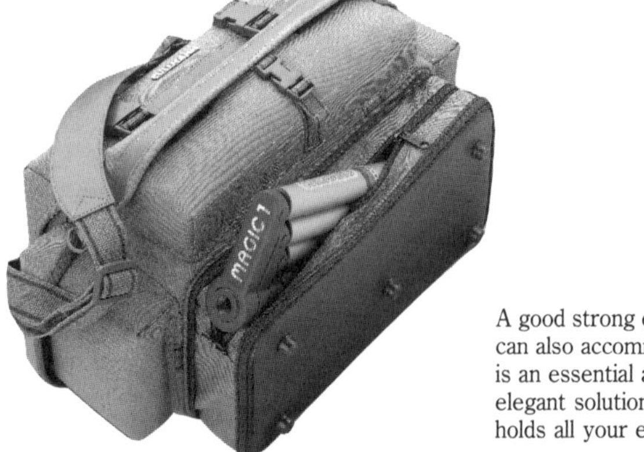

A good strong camera bag that can also accommodate a tripod is an essential accessory. This elegant solution by Cullmann holds all your equipment.

totally soft bag hangs down awkwardly and is difficult to carry. The padded sides and dividers are offered as standard with all bags these days to give reasonable protection against knocks. Removable dividers are the most practical. To install your equipment, take the dividers out, arrange your camera, etc. and then insert the dividers.

Tip: If you already have a bag, but it is not sufficiently waterproof, take a plastic bag with you. In emergencies you can wrap the bag in the plastic one. It may not look exactly elegant but it is better than getting your precious equipment wet.

Camera Cases: Canon offer these for the EOS in different sizes to accommodate the camera and a lens.

— Model S for the EOS with EF 50mm, f/1.8 lens
— Model M for the EOS with EF 35-70mm, f/3.5-4.5 lens
— Model LL for the EOS with EF 25-105mm, f/3.5-4.5 lens

These cases are suitable for photographers who have just one camera with one lens. The advantage is that the

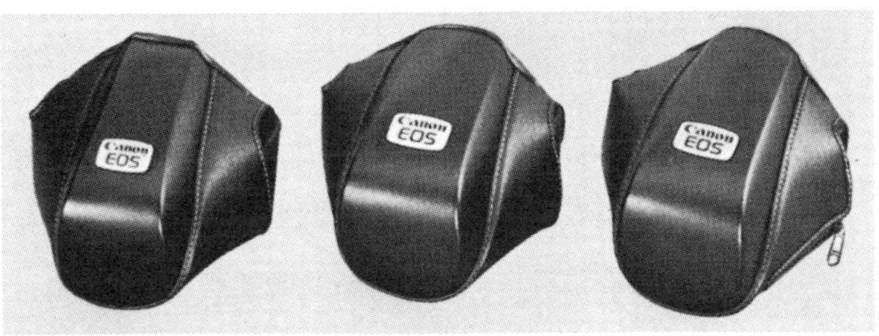

Canon offer camera cases in three sizes for the EOS.

camera is reasonably protected but the bag is easy to open to get the camera out and take a shot.

If you intend to take a lot of pictures, you might find such a case more of a hindrance than a help. Where do you put it? You'll need large pockets or a bag. A better alternative is to carry the camera without a case and to stow it away in a camera bag after you have finished.

Tripod: Sooner or later you will have to invest in a tripod. For long exposures it is absolutely essential to use a tripod. Sometimes it is undesirable to use a flash as it destroys the mood of a scene or it is not allowed.

A tripod offers other advantages for unhurried shots when you are at your leisure to arrange the subject and camera. It is sometimes difficult to find the right frame, even if the shutter speed would allow hand-held shooting.

The difficult question when buying a tripod is; do I buy something light and portable or do I need a heavy and rigid one? To start with I would recommend a light, compact tripod that can be carried around, perhaps even a small tabletop tripod. If you find that you use it quite often and that it is not rigid enough, then you may decide on buying a heavier unit. The worst thing is to buy something in between that is too heavy to carry around but not rigid enough to stand up to every job.

I would also like to remind you of the existence of monopods. These are now rather difficult to find. A

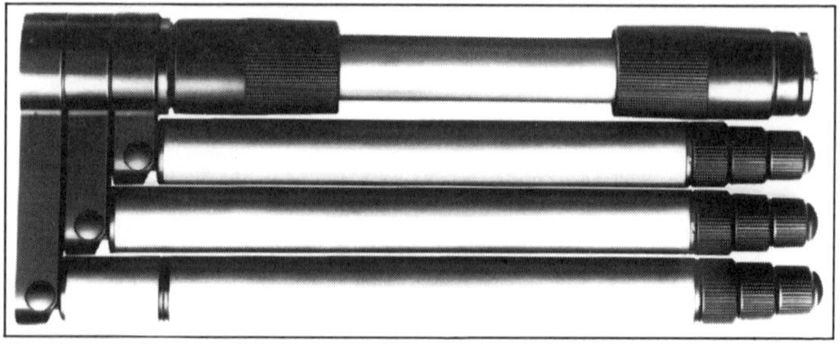

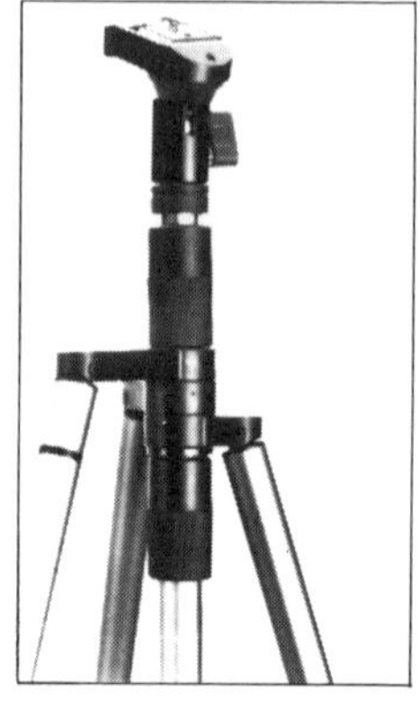

The Magic 2 tripod by Cullmann. It can be folded up and stored at the bottom of a reasonably roomy camera bag. It extends to just under 1.5m and is quite stable at this height. The centre column and tripod shaft can be assembled as a monopod.

monopod is particularly suitable for use with the EOS, especially with telephoto lenses where a tripod is inconvenient, as it helps to increase the likelihood of sharp pictures by up to about two stops. The camera can be moved almost as easily as if held unaided, but it is reasonably well supported even if the **P** blinks in the viewfinder. If you find that your main problem is camera shake and that you cannot afford, say, the expensive but super-fast EF 300mm, f/2.8 L lens, then you may well solve your problem by buying one of those relatively cheap monopods.

I am not saying that a tripod replaces a fast lens. For comparable shooting conditions the shutter speed will, by necessity, be slower. You may remember the f/stop sequence: 2.0 – 2.8 – 4.0 – 5.6 – 8.0 etc. Compared with the EF 100-300mm, f/5.6 the EF 300mm, f/2.8 is four times faster. This implies that, for the same brightness and fully open aperture, the shutter speed for the zoom lens would be, for example, $\frac{1}{125}$ sec., while the fixed focal length lens would offer a shutter speed of $\frac{1}{500}$ sec. The shutter speed of the fixed focal length lens is therefore always faster by two full stops. This is very useful in many situations like sports photography where the subject moves fast. The photographer may keep quite still, his camera supported on a tripod or monopod, but the picture will still be blurred because the subject moved too fast.

Water protection: Heavy and frequent rain is not unheard of in most European countries. To protect the EOS against rain is not a silly idea. You may disagree with me when I say that rainy days are also photographic days, but it is so. A rain hood is a good idea being relatively cheap and quite effective.

Filters: I have already mentioned UV and skylight filters as general protection for the front element. Other filters are a topic that can be discussed at great length. Using filters as a means to produce better pictures, understanding their effects and using them for the right subject, is the correct way. To do this, you need experience and this can only be gained through experimenting. I suggest therefore; buy one or two filters and shoot away. One word of caution however; don't risk any important shots, take these as usual without any filter as you never know how they will turn out with one of these special effect filters. You could always take two pictures, one with, one without a filter. In this way you could build up your own archive to be used in future for particular projects. The general guidelines to the use of filters may be summarized as follows:

To show the scene as it was:
A filter is used to show the scene as well as possible, but

it is not noticeable in the final photograph that a filter was employed. As discussed previously, what the eye sees and what the film sees are not always the same. The deep blue sky reproduced as washed-out blue in the photograph, or the colours are not shown as intense and glowing as they were in reality. This could be due to the fact that the colour temperature of the light was different from the colour temperature for which the film is balanced.

The point here is not to get an absolutely true picture that has no bias towards one or another colour. Nor am I saying that we should filter out the gentle red glow of the setting sun. But if this gentle glow is really very faint it will not be seen in the picture. In this case, using a graduated red filter will help to bring out the actual colours that were present. The same can be done with a graduated blue filter or a polarising filter to reproduce the deep blue of the sky. Further filters in this category are skylight filters, conversion and light balancing filters, and colour filters for black-and-white photography.

To emphasise the statement of the photograph: The subject is not at all or only a little affected, but the filter used emphasises certain characteristics, the message is highlighted or even increased. Effects are used in a particular, predetermined way to emphasise certain aspects of the subject. A classic example in this category are diffusion filters; sunset, pastel and starburst filters are further members of this group. Filters in this category should be used carefully and sparingly. If the filter and subject don't suit each other the whole picture will be a failure.

To create a new message: The use of the filter is clearly visible. The actual subject is seen in a new and different way. This is surely the most difficult way to use filters. The task here is to represent a subject in an individual and original way, to find a new interpretation. It may also be to intensify an existing message or to make accessible to others a personal interpretation. It makes little sense, though, to simply use one of these filters on any kind of subject. Filters in this category — speed, sepia, colour starburst, coloured diffusers and dual-colour.

Filter Systems:
One type are single filters. These have a certain diameter for a particular lens and are screwed into the filter thread of the lens. More practical and versatile are filter systems. These have a filter holder of one size, with various sized screwed adapters for the different diameter filter threads. It is therefore only necessary to buy one adapter for each different lens to which the filter holder is attached. Therefore, you need not buy every type of filter for every lens in your possession. Some filter systems can even be used in combination. You could use up to 5 filters at any one time.

It is not possible to use every type of filter with some EOS lenses. The front elements of some EOS zooms move forward or backward in the lens tube and an attached filter/filter holder would obstruct this movement. To overcome this problem it is necessary to use an extension

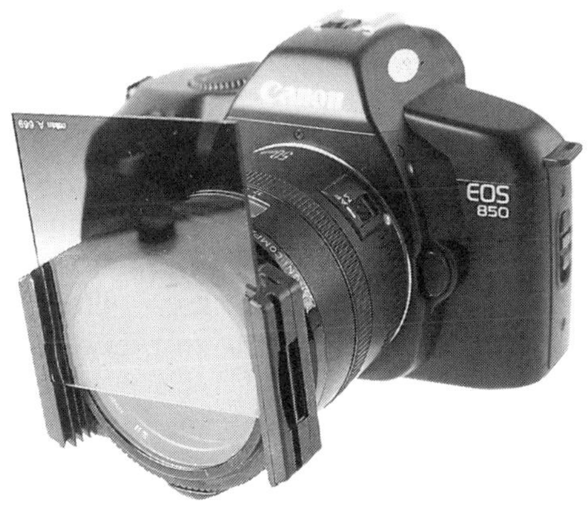

A filter system is handy as you then only need to buy one of each type of filter. Several filters can be used in combination and the filter holder can be attached by adapter to any size lens.

ring which allows free movement of the front element. Screw-in filters, on the other hand, present no problem in this respect.

Storage Systems:
The way you intend to store your pictures and negatives or slides will depend mainly on what kind you prefer. In this respect I would like to point you to the three main manufacturers of photographic accessories: Hama, Rowi and Kaiser. They offer a variety of storage systems. Their comprehensive catalogues should provide sufficient information.

The choices for the slide photographer, who projects them, are quite obvious. The slides are first sorted, any failures rejected, and the rest are stored in magazines. This system should not exceed about 1000 slides, as it would then be difficult to find a particular slide. It is often difficult to assign a particular shot to a certain subject category (holiday, family, etc.). It could get quite boring and complicated to have to project a whole series of slides in the search for a particular one. A useful alternative is slide pockets. The slides are put into pockets on a sheet and you can inspect 12 or even 24 slides at a glance.

Negatives should also be stored in negative sleeves, which may then be kept in folders. How you wish to present your prints is left to your imagination. The ways to do this are varied, from the lovingly composed picture album to the pinboard or the enlargement to poster size.

Finally I would keep a folder with the title Rubbish or a similar name. Here you could keep some representative failures. I am not suggesting a course in self-recrimination; on the contrary, these failed attempts should remind you next time you have the courage to tackle the same subject, of what went wrong last time, in order not to repeat the same mistake.

The Right Equipment for Every Situation

Now you have learnt everything about your EOS, the lenses and the accessories. You have also learnt a little about photography in general. Now is the time to decide on the right equipment for your own specific needs. Do keep in mind, however, that it is not just the equipment that takes the pictures, it is your own endeavours that will produce the results. Do not expect too much of the first series of pictures. You may be very disappointed when inspecting the first package that you receive back from the lab, depending on how critical you are, of course. The reason is quite straightforward. It is difficult to assess exactly what happens and what are the important criteria for every shot. The subject may be too small in the frame, or be too dominant, the picture could be blurred, the framing badly chosen; the reasons are innumerable.

Let's take the situation of a horse race. You may have pressed the release exactly as the horse was in full flight across the jump. The picture you actually got may be as the horse was touching the ground. The timing of such shots is very difficult. To be considered here is the photographer's, and also the camera's, reaction time, because this means that the shot will be taken perhaps a tenth of a second too late. To get the timing right, you would have to release a little earlier. By how much, depends on the camera, the reaction time of the photographer and the speed of the subject. As you can see, it is not so easy to consider all the factors and to judge them correctly. I do not wish to put you off such subjects; I am only pointing out where your mistakes may lie to help you reduce your general failure rate in the future.

These days it is no longer very difficult to decide on the right equipment. The offer of good zoom lenses at acceptable prices allows you to cover a reasonable focal length range. Two lenses would cover the entire range

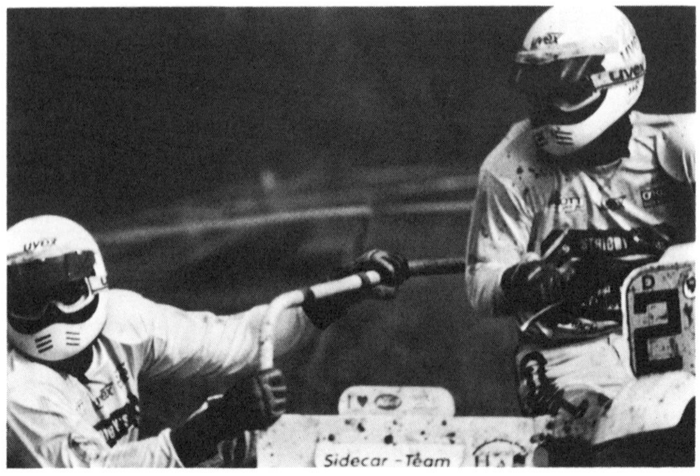

A zoom lens allows a quick transition from a general view to a detail while the photographer takes his shots from a safe distance!

from 28 to 300mm. This should be sufficient as a basic outfit. The advantage for the modern photographer is that he can freely explore a wide range of subjects. Most Canon zoom lenses offer a suitable focal length for most subjects. If you suddenly feel like taking some portraits, one or the other of your zoom lenses will offer a suitable focal length. The same will be true for most subjects.

You may ask why should you buy any fixed focal lengths at all? The answer is quite simple. If you look at the range of EOS lenses offered by Canon, then you will see at a glance; each of them is a specialist in its field. One is fast (50mm, f/1.8), the other is ideal for close-up photography (50mm, f/2.5 macro) and the third is a specialist portrait lens (135mm, f/2.8 Soft focus). In the telephoto range, too, you can find particularly fast lenses, e.g. the 300mm, f/2.8 or the 600mm, f/4.0.

For this reason I would recommend that you buy one of the standard zoom lenses to start with. This should open up a large variety of subjects which you can explore. A telephoto zoom will complement this very nicely. You will probably shoot away quite happily until, one day, you will realize that you have come upon certain limitations. To mention just two examples; despite the macro setting on most Canon zooms, you cannot get close enough to the subject or the largest aperture of the lens is not sufficient for the dusk landscapes you like to capture. This is quite normal as most enthusiastic photographers find an area of photography that is of particular interest to them. Now you should seriously consider whether your interest is really strong enough to warrant the expense of a fixed focal length lens. If the answer is 'yes', do not hesitate, otherwise you may spoil your interest and fun in photography altogether.

At the present stage of technology there are really only three good reasons why you should prefer fixed focal length lenses to zoom lenses:

1. Zoom lenses are invariably slower. For this reason you will need a fixed focal length lens for available light photography.
2. Zoom lenses have a limited close-up setting range. For real close-up photography a specialist macro lens will be a must.
3. Finally, there are still gaps that are not covered by zoom lenses; in particular in the extreme wide-angle and telephoto ranges. Canon offer no zoom lenses below 28mm or above 300mm, although there may be alternatives from other manufacturers.

Outside the range of zoom lenses Canon offer fixed focal length lenses.

Suitable Equipment

Thanks to the existence of good zoom lenses, it is no problem compiling a suitable list of equipment for a wide range of applications. A smaller starter set could be something like this; your EOS camera (naturally!), one of the zoom lenses, camera bag, cleaning set, UV filter to protect the lens, lens hood and a flashgun. If you have an EOS 750 you won't need a separate flashgun as the integrated flash will cope with most ordinary situations.

The first important accessories are a puffer brush, lens cleaning tissues and pressurized air to clean the lenses. Then you may wish to add a filter holder with adapter for the lenses in your possession and a polarising filter and perhaps one or two special effect filters.

With regard to films I would recommend one or two each of slow, medium speed and fast films so that you may assess the grain and resolution capabilities of the different films and also their range of applications. I suggest: ISO 50/18°, ISO 100/21° and ISO 1000/31°. Perhaps you wish to include colour print and slide films and a black-and-white film. Now you can experiment with the available material to your heart's content.

Tip: Keep your films in the fridge or even in the freezer. Stored this way they will keep in good condition even beyond the recommended expiry dates. Before use leave them out for a few hours to warm up.

A larger equipment set should contain two zoom lenses. For example the EF 28-70mm, f/3.5-4.5 plus the EF 70-210mm, f/4.0, or a similar combination, ranging from the wide-angle to the telephoto range. With this outfit you can cover almost every conceivable situation.

Close-ups: The macro setting on your lens (available on most EF lenses) should be sufficient for a start. Depending on the lens, you can shoot subjects between 20 and 40cm in full-format. The 50mm, f/2.5 Macro is a specialist lens for photographers who like to concentrate on close-up photography and who expect a great deal with regard to sharpness, contrast and absence of curvature of field. This lens is the only one offered by Canon giving a reproduction scale of 1:1.

Now you should be equipped for every eventuality. Should your interests develop, let's say in the direction of extreme wide-angle shots, then you should heed my advice; always move from the general to the specific. It is not very sensible immediately to go and buy a fisheye lens just because you have seen an amazing picture taken with such a lens. Consider whether or not a 28mm or 24mm would be more useful. The fisheye can be added later if you really intend becoming a wide-angle fanatic.

With the all the considerations of which equipment to buy you should not forget that you have bought your camera to take good pictures. Not even the best equipment can do this for you. It is the photographer who makes the pictures so all that is left now is to wish you good luck and have fun!